A 20,000% Gain in Real Estate

A True Story About the Ups and Downs from Wall Street to Real Estate Leading Up to Phenomenal Returns

10-Digit ISBN 1-59113-784-5
13-Digit ISBN 978-1-59113-784-9

Printed in the United States of America.

This publication is designed to provide general information regarding the subject matter covered. However, laws and practices often vary from state to state and are subject to change. Because each factual situation is different, specific strategies should be tailored to the particular circumstance. For this reason, the reader is advised to consult with his or her own advisor regarding the individual's situation.

The author has taken reasonable precautions in the preparation of this book and believes the facts presented in the book are accurate as of the date it was written. However, neither the author nor the publisher assume any responsibility for any errors or omissions. The author and publisher specifically disclaim any liability resulting from the use or application of the information contained in this book, and the information is not intended to serve as legal, financial or other professional advice related to individual situations.

Booklocker.com, Inc.
2005

A 20,000% Gain in Real Estate

A True Story About the Ups and Downs from Wall Street to Real Estate Leading Up to Phenomenal Returns

Kevin Kingston

This book is dedicated to
my wife Lina who stood beside me
and encouraged me through all the ups
and downs mentioned herein and many more.

Contents

Introduction

My first real estate purchase was a $215,000 single-family home in Hartsdale, New York. Although not intended to be an investment, this purchase would help influence and fund my transition from Wall Street to real estate. The date was June 1997, and the down payment was $15,000, part of which was a loan from my mother. Seven years and nine months later this $15k has exploded to over $3 million in equity through refinancing and purchasing investment properties. The amazing thing is, I never put another dime of my own money, other than this $15,000, into purchasing another property. This story will give you the play-by-play description, including the severe ups and violent downs, of life as a stockbroker in the '90s to life as a real estate investor in the present. I'll share the craziness and cycles that go hand in hand with life on Wall Street as a million-dollar producer during one of the greatest booms in history. Then, in the midst of the greatest financial meltdown the NASDAQ has ever seen, we'll walk through an extremely timely transition to a real estate investor after having been completely wiped out both monetarily and mentally from the technology stock market collapse.

My goal is to shed some light on a few indisputable truths that I stumbled upon that can, without a doubt, have life-changing implications if implemented properly. I have searched through hundreds of books on trading, investing, and real estate and studied the biographies of a myriad of empire builders to heads of industry. I have passed along bits of information from each, along with quotes, philosophies, and agendas, and explained a few very simple processes that can lead to extraordinary results.

This book is intended to act as a guide for future investors. I'd like nothing more than to pass along, in an easy-to-read format, a few simple ideas, like my amplified-return concept, to which I've devoted a chapter to explain in detail how, with the use of leverage, it is possible to magnify even the smallest percent moves in a market, specifically the real estate market. I've done my best to explain cycles and how they affect the people involved, using examples of those—mainly me—who get caught up and swept away by them. Best of all, I'll prove without a shadow of a doubt that down does not mean out!

PART I

Chapter One
Starting Out: The Windmill and Back Again

"Fortune is not satisfied with inflicting one calamity."
–Publilus Syrus (First century B.C.)
Maxim 274

To give you a full prospective on my investment history, I will start with the story in April 1990, fifteen years ago. This is when I passed my series 7 exam and started my Wall Street career. The series 7 is the exam a stockbroker must pass to be legally able to sell securities to investors. Because I was only 19, it was a little difficult getting hired at a large, well-known, respectable brokerage firm. I did what seemed natural and took the local phone book and started calling all of the stock brokerage firms within a twenty-minute drive of my parents' home, where I was living at the time. I started in the back of the book and finally got Bob Crossman, the owner of the Windmill Group Inc., on the phone. Somehow I finagled an interview and then talked my way into a job (with no salary) at the worldwide headquarters in Armonk, New York, which happened to also be the only office of the Windmill Group.

Oddly enough, at about the same time, I was in discussions with Weichert Realtors in White Plains, New York, to start as a real estate salesperson. I think they may have even had a formal training program with some sort of starting salary or draw. I turned this opportunity down because I figured Wall Street was where the real money was.

Both my mother and father were teachers. My mom was a retired substitute that had a master's in education, and my father had his Ph.D. in forensic science from Berkeley, California, and was a professor at John Jay College of Criminal Justice in Manhattan. So the idea of me not devoting 100 percent of my time to college and then to higher education did not exactly sit well with them, but all in all, they stood behind my decisions.

I can remember starting out at the Windmill Group and meeting the gang: Fred Adams, Shebna Olson, Kathy and Tom Hanlon. The girls, receptionists, and sales assistant were nice as can be, and Fred and Tom stood ready to answer all of my questions and tell me stories of their wild experiences over the last twenty-plus years on Wall Street. What my job really boiled down to was me sitting in a corner with a phone book and S&P stock guide in hand trying to find something to sell and someone to sell it to. I loved it! It was a challenge, and I did it. I did it and did it and did it. Day in and day out; I was hammering out twelve- to fourteen-hour days throughout the spring and summer, with the windows open and the birds chirping in the lovely Armonk setting. I had a fierce determination to succeed.

Tom Hanlon, a fiftysomething broker who was seemingly winding down but still going through the daily motions of attentively keeping an eye on the quote machine, acted as my research department and market strategist. His favorite stock, Ancon Genetics (ANCN), was at $.10 (ten cents) and going to $100 soon. He guaranteed it and suggested I load up as fast as I can, which I fortunately did not do.

For the summer of 1990 I plugged along trying to find something worthwhile to sell and cold-calling to open accounts. My first account bought a closed-end fund issued by one of the mutual fund companies and some Disney stock. It was a great thrill to create business from nothing. The main theme for new brokers is to build a book of clients and gather assets. I worked day and night until 10 p.m. and Saturdays as well. It was a very slow start, but I was determined to make a go of it.

My girlfriend, Lina, was very supportive, and most nights I would stop by her house on the way home for a visit. Most of these visits included a gourmet dinner, usually saved for me in the oven. Lina's parents are from the Abruzzi region of Italy, and her mother is an unbelievable cook. Both of Lina's uncles—her mother's brothers—are top chefs who own restaurants in Europe: one brother, Celestino, owns an eatery in Sulmona, Italy, and the other, Amedeo, owns a few in Germany. They both attended top culinary schools in the Abruzzi region. Eating at Lina's was always an experience. Everything is homemade—the pasta, bread, sauce, you name it. In the back of the house is a little room that could be confused with little Sicily, with prosciutto, sausage, cheeses, peppers, and spices all hanging from the ceiling. I think Lina enjoyed the fact that I was a hard worker who was driven to succeed. God knows her family tested that theory every year at the end of August by putting me to work when it was tomato sauce time. They would load up with nine to ten bushels of tomatoes and have a weekend marathon–type event centered on jarring enough sauce to last the rest of the year. It was hard work, but well worth it.

After a great dinner, I would go home and rest up for the next day, when I would be back in the saddle again bright and early. Calling and calling and making very little progress. Until one day Freddie Ballou walked in. Fred was a real dealmaker. He was discussing with Bob the idea of opening another office for the Windmill Group, in New Jersey. Fred operated in an interesting, sort of mysterious way. At least for a brand-new, fresh-out-of-the box, newly licensed broker trying to figure out the business on his own. Fred took me under his wing and gave me the guidance I needed so desperately. He taught me a few tricks about systems and procedures, like keeping index cards on prospects and having more than one idea for prospects on every call. He also taught me some selling techniques, such as capturing someone's attention on the phone by revealing the yield on a bond right at the outset.

Fred wanted to set up a bond department with me as the sole salesman, at least until we got it off the ground and it started to grow. The idea was to grow the business, but as usually happens on Wall Street, greed prevailed and the idea fell apart.

Fred introduced me to Bruce Barber, a housing bond specialist whose job was to buy bonds to resell and to update me on them daily to sell to clients. This worked out well for a while. I started opening accounts, and I was actually becoming quite good at it.

Soon Fred struck up a deal with another firm in New York City, where he most likely promised to bring over a thriving bond department. The extent of the promises, I am not exactly sure. I joined him in this new venture, and we set up shop on 37th Street and Park Avenue in New York City, with a floor all to ourselves in a beautiful brownstone turned into offices. This was very exciting, as all new ventures are for me. We, meaning me tagging along with Fred, got right back into the groove and continued right where we had left off. In addition to opening accounts, I would show a daily bond list to the rest of the brokers, in essence acting as their bond department. These brokers had zero interest in bonds; they were hard-core penny stock brokers. This was 1991, and most of them had come from Blinder Robinson or other penny stock firms, where they were used to . . . well, let's just call it a "different type of business."

It was really something to build a business with Fred. He was full of ideas and encouragement. I would cold-call all day, trying to open accounts and sell bonds, and he would go off and have five-hour lunches—or meetings, as he called them. Then, in the evening, he would pop in and see how much we made for the day. When I brought up the fact that I was working all day while he was out doing God knows what, he said I was starting to sound like his ex-wife. New York was exciting, though, and most nights we would stop for a few beers on our way up Third Avenue so he could resume his pep talk and lay out his grandiose plans for our operation.

I soon started noticing how much the other brokers were making by selling stock. These weren't blue chips, I assure you. Whenever I spoke to Fred about this, he told me that was the dark side and to stay away if I wanted to last in the business. I was intrigued by the amount of money these guys were making, but Fred assured me that they were doing more harm than good. These guys would have a big commission month and then disappear to the Bahamas for a week or two, sometimes calling the manager for a plane ticket back because they had spent all their money.

One Monday, Fred and I showed up for work ready to rock and roll, only to find the door to the office kicked in and everything gone. I mean everything: the computers, the phones cut right out of the wall, the TV—even my book of clients. Everything. We had been robbed, and we had a feeling it was an inside job. I was not sticking around with a bunch of rouge brokers in that office another day longer.

So that was that. I went back to the Windmill Group, and lucky for me, Bob gave me another shot. I also worked out a pretty good deal. I was able to work from home and keep 80 percent of my commission. I was also attending college, taking business courses. It was a great job. Work from home on my own schedule, hit the phones when I want, hit the gym when I could, or just take the day off.

Selling tax-free bonds was easy enough, but selling high-yield bonds was even easier—in fact, the higher the yield, the easier the sale. Bond investors wanted YIELD. When the bonds Bruce would show me to sell didn't have enough kick, I would go through the Blue List myself. The Blue List is a book of municipal bonds for sale by dealers all over the country. Here I am, twenty years old, working from home (most of the time in boxer shorts), calling dealers looking for high-yield bonds. They all had a story. This area is being redeveloped, or this hospital has a special issue. Between the story and the yield, it was usually enough to get most bond buyers tempted, even if the rating was not quite investment-grade.

Then came my first blowup. I sold $100,000 worth of "special situation" high-yield municipal bonds that defaulted within a few months of selling them. It turns out that the dealer who sold them to me, who in turn sold them to a few clients, had a good idea they were going to default, which meant they would stop paying the interest—imagine that. So after us bringing the dealer to arbitration, and the clients bringing us to arbitration, the clients got most of their money back—mostly from me. As it turned out, there was no real regulation on dealer-to-dealer transactions. This group bought these bonds at 40 to 60 cents on the dollar and sold them to us close to par (100 cents on the dollar), thus making $40,000 to $60,000 profit on the transaction. I in turn marked the bonds up 3 points or thereabouts, making roughly $3,000 on the sale. I think the settlement, after months of finger-pointing and frustration, cost me close to $40,000. Needless to say, this was enough of high-yield or "special situation" bonds for me, at least for a while.

During this time (1991), I was enjoying months where I brought in $15,000 to $25,000 in commission and keeping 80 percent of it. I remember going to the local Bank of New York in Armonk and cashing an $18,000 check. When the teller saw the transaction, she said, "Wouldn't you like to deposit this?" I replied, "No, hundreds please." This was a great time. This lasted for a year or so. Going to class, coming home and doing a little business, then heading to the gym. Since I was working from home, I did not have the benefit of the Windmill's in-house market gurus Tom and Fred. This is when I started to read trading books. Over the course of my time on Wall Street, I read dozens.

Some of the first trading and investing books I read were about William O'Neil's CANSLIM methodology. CANSLIM stands for:

C = Current earnings growth over, say, 20 percent growth
A = Annual earnings, strong growth as well
N = Something new in the marketplace
S = Shares outstanding, the less the better
L = Leading Industry Group
I = Institutional holdings, the lower the better
M =Overall market needs to be favorable

William O'Neil is a stockbroker turned newspaper publisher. He has a very interesting career, for anyone who enjoys reading about successful people, as I do! He started and continues to run *Investors Business Daily* or *IBD,* as it is usually referred. The paper also has a daily spotlight section offering a one-page biography of extremely successful achievers. Reading about these people and what they overcame has helped me get through some real tough times.

Another interesting investor, Nicolas Darvis, wrote a book titled *How I Made $2,000,000 in the Stock Market*. He explains how he used a similar system to CANSLIM. He called it a Techno-Fundamentalist approach: a mix of technical (paying attention to charts, price, volume, resistance, and support levels) and fundamental strategies (looking at the underlying business, including the ratios, such as price to book value and earning-per-share growth). In addition, this system also incorporates the "something-new factor," which is some new product or technology that will catch on fast and furious. He believed and subsequently proved this theory by making more than $2,000,000 in less than two years. He contends that you can find that "something new" simply by looking at the action of the stock and the volume coming into it. He based his decisions solely on these two criteria. He would not even allow his brokers to call him; he just had them send telegrams of the day's price activity.

This information encouraged me to open new accounts to buy and sell stocks to earn commission and to put money in my account to trade with. I remember having 52 weeks' worth of *IBD* and *Barron's* spread out all over my living-room floor, looking for some type of pattern to base my trading on. I always came up with something—either a stock that just broke out of a trading range or some new product that I thought would be a big hit. The thing is, in a rising market, almost everything rises. All boats rise with a rising tide. This gives investors a false sense of security. It also gives stockbrokers a feeling that is hard to explain. A sort of euphoria with a mix of adrenaline that, when combined with a type A personality, creates an almost toxic mix for stockbrokers, which we in turn pass right through to the costumers. There is no doubt that salesmanship rises with excitement, and excitement rises with a rising market. The faster the market rises, the higher the level of excitement, and the higher the level of salesmanship. This is the essence of what would lead to some wild and crazy cycles in my Wall Street career. This excitement is contagious and addictive. We earn more commission. People send us larger checks. People put more money into stocks than they normally would have. This, of course, adds to the overall excitement, which builds on itself. When the market finally turns, it is very hard to accept, and because of the rush associated with rising prices, it's difficult to let go of the very addictive feeling.

At least for me, as an easily excitable person, this is a hard predicament to be in. I get extremely caught up in the hype. As you can imagine, when the market finally came tumbling down, I was in denial. By the way, these ups and downs get intensified with the use of margin. An example of margin is buying $50,000 worth of stock for $25,000. When the market goes up, you make twice as much money, and when it comes down, you lose twice as much (a.k.a. leverage). Leverage is a magical and dangerous concept where the implications are mind-boggling. Of course, a good chunk of my clients were margined up to the hilt when my first experience of a downturn came, and the pain was almost unbearable. I remember sitting in class at Westchester Community College and not being able to hear a word the professor was saying. All I could think about were my poor clients and what a bad broker I was not to get them out of the market as it continued to sink. I literally walked out of class, with people asking me if I was all right. I was soaking wet from sweat, pale white, and hunched over a bit because I thought I might be ill. My personal account had gotten wiped out first because it was the most margined. That was okay with me; it was my clients for which I was most concerned.

The only people who could console or even relate to what I was going through were the gang at Windmill. Tom, Freddie A., and the girls. Tom and Freddie A. told me they had been through it many times and it's never fun. They even had little skits to try and cheer me up. Then there was Pat's, the local pub. We spent many an afternoon there drinking beers and commiserating. I don't think this downturn hit them quite as hard as it hit me, but they were there for me just the same. And boy did I need them! I would get lost in my despair. A few times I would get on my motorcycle, a Yamaha FZR 600, and drive as fast as it would go, not really caring about much, almost wanting to crash. The pain of losing someone else's money is monumental. What really hurt most was that Lina, now my wife, had opened an account for her mother, who could in no way afford to lose the type of money she did. I just couldn't get it out of my mind.

To top things off, Centecor (CNTO), a biotechnology company that I had a large position in, gapped down almost in half. When a stock gapes down, it just opens lower; there is no chance to sell between the price it closes at and the price that it opened for trading. This happens because of an order imbalance, with more sell orders than buy orders, usually because of bad news. This brought the final blow to my aggressive accounts that were hanging on by a thread. Finally I took my book of clients to the office and handed it to Bob and said, "I can't take it. This is not for me. Take this book. I'm done." And then I walked out. Well, Bob would have none of that. He marched right up behind me and said, "Get in there and be a man and face the music. Call those people and explain what happened." It was the hardest thing I ever had to do up to this point in my life. I listened to Bob, and those words stayed with me till this day. Sure enough, it felt better after I spoke to all the clients. Everyone took it better than I had expected.

In spite of all the feelings, you need to try to stay positive to your clients. Assure them that eventually the market will pick back up. The problem is that if they were margined, they may have lost most of the money in the account, and it's almost impossible for the account to come back.

It was a long summer; time passes, and life goes on. I worked on leaving the pain and memories of sinking stocks and dwindling accounts behind me. I took some time off and painted some houses with my buddies, as well as spent more time in the gym. When working from home, it's easy to avoid actually doing work when times are tough. I was still making a few bucks a month, but nothing like when the market was hot.

Chapter Two
Greenwich, Connecticut, and the Program

"That which does not kill us makes us stronger."
–Fredrich Nietzsche (1844–1900)

Fred Ballou, being the type of person that likes to put things together again, convinced me we could come back from the mishap on 37th Street. He purchased new computers, phones, fax machines, and even opened an office on Putnam Avenue in Greenwich, Connecticut, the town in which he resided. This time around it was Fred, David Barron, and myself. David worked for Fred several years before, when he ran his own brokerage firm. They did well in the '80s with high-yield municipal bonds. That operation came to an end for some reason, probably due to greed, misjudgment, and excessive risk.

Here we were, the three of us in a two-room office in Greenwich, right next to the YMCA where Dave was living at the time. Fred had a plan. It went something like this: We use Telescan, a program that allows users to search through more than 8,000 companies for those that meet a certain criteria. This is fairly common these days, but in the early '90s it was unique. We would look for stocks that showed good earnings, an unusual spike in volume, and a good chart pattern. I would call their old clients and explain how the program works and open accounts. Telescan would help us find situations because of the volume before any news was announced. We could do searches for stocks whose volume suddenly spiked. If the volume started coming in and there was no news and the company had an improving earnings picture, chances were it was good for a trade. It worked well, and we were fairly successful.

The concept was to get as many accounts ready for action on a daily basis as possible. I would explain that we would do the research at night and find stocks as they were just starting to move. We would aim not to put more than 10 percent of anyone's account in any one position. This way we would have at least 10 and as many as 20 different positions in an account. Almost daily, there would be a position bought or sold. We would try to keep the losses small, usually between 7 percent and 13 percent, and let the profitable stocks run until they ran out of steam. So if you have twenty-five accounts in the program and have a trade to do every day or every other day and charge an average of $200 per trade, that is about $5,000 in commission on the sell and another $5,000 on the buy.

Within months we were back in the routine. I was hitting the phones all day, and Fred would show up at closing time to count the tickets and persuade me to go next door for a margarita. But Fred was soon distracted by a multimillion-dollar deal with some Europeans and lost interest in our little operation. I had approximately 100 accounts and was now able to go to a larger, wirehouse-type firm, which would otherwise never hire a young twentysomething-year-old without a college degree and no business connections.

Starting out, I had two main choices: Take the route I did, which had no formal training program and zero corporate resources to back any expenses I incurred, with the exception of a phone and sometimes quotes, or start on the "dark side," as Fred called it. By this he was referring to the dozens of small chophouses or penny stock firms that were flourishing at the time. When interviewing with these firms, all they would talk about is the six-figure months they were having and all the cars or exotic trips they were taking. Not a word about the real business of investing and making clients wealthy.

Chapter Three
Off to PaineWebber and Prudential Securities

"Always bear in mind that your own resolution to succeed is more important than any other one thing."

–Abraham Lincoln

In 1993 I made my move to PaineWebber. Ken Mahoney urged me to come in and talk to the manager, Tom Reichet. I did, and Tom hired me on the spot. What a difference a book of business makes. The referral from Ken helped out tremendously as well. Ken and I met in early 1990 on Paradise Island Beach in the Bahamas. I was there with Lina and six of her girlfriends. Ken was with a mutual friend of ours, Mike Sacco. I guess Ken figured he could either pal around with Mike or hang around with me and seven girls. I was studying for my series 7 test at the time and fired off nonstop questions to both Ken and Mike. We were sitting on the beach, and I was drilling them with questions about complex option strategies, margin requirements, yield curves, T Bills, and inflation. It was comical. Ken and I remain the best of friends to this day.

Most large brokerage firms sent their top producers on an annual trip to a five-star resort hotel. At PaineWebber the production level to make the trip depended on your level of service or years in the business. I am not sure what the cutoff was, but I made the trip my first year. What a trip it was. They sent the top percentage of producers to the Phoenician Golf Resort in Scottsdale, Arizona, for four days. Sitting by the pool all day, having jumbo shrimp cocktails and beluga caviar with champagne, was a blast. On the second night, they flew in Donna Summer for the '70s disco theme night. Lina and I enjoyed the trip tremendously. These getaways really encouraged you to be a top producer. I hung out with Ken Mahoney and Mario Ferrari, another broker that I became closer friends with after the trip. The girls enjoyed the spa while the guys enjoyed the bar. We must have had over twenty grand worth of caviar, shrimp, and champagne. I was sure we would hear about it when we got back to New York, but there was not a peep.

I stayed at PaineWebber for about a year and increased my business to the mid $200k level and was offered a $60,000 bonus to move to Prudential Securities. I stayed with Prudential for nearly three years, getting my business up to roughly $350k a year. I wasn't making a fortune for my clients, but I wasn't losing their fortune either. I, on the other hand, lost every penny of the bonus money and most of my monthly paycheck. At the large brokerage firms, you are on a payout, or paid a percentage of your total commissions for the month. The payout depends on the level of commission. At the $350k level, you are somewhere between 40 and 50 percent. This is good money for a single guy in his early twenties. This type of money made it hard to put limits on myself. I would throw money into the market, basically gambling on my own account—and losing most of it. At this point, I was leasing a black 745I BMW, renting an apartment, and enjoying my new boat—a 30-foot Regal Commodore.

Spending money like this was fun but unfulfilling. At PaineWebber and then Prudential Securities, my book of clients would double and then double again. For some reason I wanted more excitement: I wanted to build up my team of junior brokers and cold callers to ten or twenty people. The larger firms wanted to keep things smaller and simpler without rocking the boat. I kept telling myself that at least I'm building a foundation and a reputation with my newsletter, "The Kingston Letter," and a radio show called *Wall Street Wrap-up,* which I co-hosted with my friend and coworker TJ. We would interview CEOs of local publicly traded companies. These helped us open accounts and add to our credibility. We would mix up the show with analysts, money managers, and some figure heads like Larry Wachtell at Prudential and Joe Battipaglia, who was the chief market strategist at Gruntal and Company.

I guess I was just looking for more energy, more excitement, and more passion. There was no place better to find these things than in an office in midtown Manhattan with young, energetic brokers.

Chapter Four
The Move Back to New York City

"In adversity assume the countenance of prosperity, and in prosperity moderate the temper and desires."
–Titus Livius (59 B.C. – A.D. 17)

Throughout the last few years in the business, I was determined to build something, to create a business of more than just a stockbroker with a few assistants. I was constantly pushing to hire more junior brokers or trainees, in essence to create a large team. However, I couldn't get my managers to back me up on this idea. They would agree to a sales assistant and one junior broker, at best. In my mind, it was simple to understand that by hiring junior brokers, I could leverage my productivity, open more accounts, contact more people, and thus better service our existing clients. I never expected the firm to pay for these junior brokers. I would gladly have paid them myself, because I believed it would pay off in spades in the long run. More accounts, more assets, and better service equals happier clients as well as more commissions. It works, I can assure you. I had a great junior broker when I was working at Prudential Securities. His name was Dan Vitek. He opened more than fifty accounts, some of which were very lucrative. I was looking to grow; I was looking for leverage. The fact that Prudential was not willing to help me grow—my way—forced me to look at other firms.

During my search for a new firm, I came across a hip young manager from Gruntal and Company, located in the Third Avenue office. I convinced three other brokers to meet with him as well. TJ, Scott Jerutis, Rich Rynik, and I all made the move within the next few months. My upfront bonus was $80,000. Three of us were given the corner office on the third floor at 605 3rd Avenue. It was a nice big office that had a great view of Docks Bar and Restaurant on the corner of 40th and 3rd, where we would meet after work to strategize. Overall, we had a great time while growing our businesses. TJ, Scott, and I shared the office; it was big enough to accommodate four additional people. That extra space was being saved for the junior brokers. The agreement was that for every $250,000 I generated in commissions, the firm would pay for a junior broker.

Rich worked in the bullpen. The bullpen is in the center of the office, where forty or so cubicles were comprised to house the lower-producing brokers, who worked the phones. Once they increased their business, they moved to an office. Rich is the type of guy that enjoyed roughing it. He ended up buying our 30-foot Regal Commodore and living on it. He changed the name from Double Trouble to The Day Trader and promptly moved his tiki bar from his living room to the boat, where he works half the time. Therefore, working in the bullpen was no big deal to him.

The Third Avenue Gruntal office had a reputation for hiring younger, more aggressive, up-and-coming types. There were lots of super-aggressive stock traders in this office—guys building large positions in story stocks, others loading up on takeover targets. It was a very exciting place, and we loved it. We settled into our corner office and went right to work. There was one junior broker working alongside each of us. That put six people in the office cranking it out. When the market heated up, our junior brokers would be like sprinters, running order tickets to the wire room. They would literally go all day nonstop from 9:30 a.m., when the market opened, to 4 p.m., when the closing bell rang. The junior brokers counted the minutes until the closing bell. When it rang, they would collapse from exhaustion. Scott and I would light up cigars while TJ fired up his pipe. Then we would have a drink and review the day's events. This was the most fun I had on Wall Street.

A Wall Street tradition is to cut off the tie of a junior broker when they opened their first account. This was always a great day for the office. The junior broker would do a dance on the desks for all of Third Avenue to see. On the flipside, another tradition, but one held only by our office, was to send one of the junior brokers out to get a few bottles of champagne when the Dow Jones Industrials would fall a few hundred points. We figured we may as well make the best of it. What else could we do?

There were many interesting brokers, and for the most part, we all got along great. Our office always had visitors chatting about the market or looking for a good trading idea. In the office next to us was a broker named Mo. He had more than 100,000 shares of some computer company in his book, and when it went from $1 to $35 per share, he threw a party at some trendy downtown bar. He earned huge commissions that month. Right next to Mo were the Greeks, Louie and Lambrose. They were brothers-in-law and always had a good story to tell about some company or other that was on the brink of exploding. Another charismatic broker at Gruntal was Angelo Pomes. He had several European clients, and more often than not, I would see Angelo in front of the building pacing back and forth, having a cigarette and a coffee, with a cell phone glued to his ear, chattering in Italian. His famous phrase was, "I just picked up five thousand shares" or "I just let them have five thousand shares." The word in our office was that during some months Angelo was beating the market by five or ten to one. Angelo was a super-aggressive trader who always had a good trading idea. In all, I figure there were close to seventy-five brokers in the office.

At this time, I was very close to buying a brownstone in the Murray Hill section of New York City. You could purchase one for around a million dollars back then. I had managed to save some money during my time at Prudential, and when added to the bonus money I received when I made my move to Gruntal, I could have managed the down payment. However, I decided to wait. The market was on fire, and my account was going strong, and it seemed like there was no stopping it. Not long after we got situated at Gruntal, the foreign-currency crisis kicked in. One developing country after another would re-value their currency, and this sent the U.S. stock market into a tailspin. The Asian contagion, as it was being called, took care of any thoughts of the brownstone; it cleaned my account right out. Ahhh . . . the ups and downs of Wall Street.

One notable junior broker and personal friend that worked for me at the time was Mike Zerilli. He was a Mount Vernon police officer who was on leave to explore the brokerage business. He worked diligently and took notes on his lead cards as if writing a police report. Although the market was sinking, he still provided us with humor. One of his antics was to call the phone booth on the corner of 40th Street and Third Avenue when someone was either walking by or waiting to cross the street. We had a perfect view from our third-floor corner office, enabling us to make out facial expressions and enjoy the full reaction of our "victims." If they answered the phone, he would say things like, "Hello. Please don't say anything. This is the Special Division of Surveillance, and we need your help. Please walk straight to the coffee vendor and tell him, 'The crow flew over the cuckoo's nest.' He will hand you a package, and you must run it to that white van parked on the corner." More than half the people would do it with no questions asked. The coffee vendor, who didn't understand English very well, would get so frustrated. It was the funniest thing we had ever seen. We laughed so hard it hurt.

After having so much fun and making so much money because of strong markets, it's hard to face the reality of a sinking market. You never really know how far the market will fall. So unless you have a strict sell discipline and get right out when things start to turn south, you try to ride it out. Brokers are a hopeful bunch who tend to be optimists, especially after a year with a great market. Soon the euphoria in the Third Avenue office turned to despair. The market turned, and turned fast. You never can tell just how bad things will get when you're in the thick of it. Of course, hindsight is 20/20, but when you're going through it, it goes something like this: After the first downturn, you hope it's just a hiccup. Then, after more declines, you wonder why the hell you are still in the market and why you didn't sell. And finally, when the decline is nearly over, the super-aggressive accounts are wiped out and everyone else is stunned into inaction. My personal account, which fell into this super-aggressive category, was one of the first to be completely annihilated.

My mother was critical of the amount of money I wasted. She said, "Look at this limo you're driving (referring to the black 745i).

You don't even own it. You rent an apartment and have no savings." Her advice was to buy a house. So I did. I called a local Realtor and bought the very first house she showed me. Looking back, I think the Realtor went into shock. But when it was time to close, I had no money. I lost it all in the market during a downturn. I ended up cleaning out my retirement savings and borrowing the rest from my mother. I don't think she understood where all my money went, but she was glad I bought the house nonetheless. It was June of 1997, and the house cost $215,000. The only money I ever put toward the purchase of real estate was the $15,000 down payment.

Here we were in Painesville again on Wall Street. This time the market came down fast, and it was over quickly. The money was gone, and that was that. I figured I could either start over, work hard and make the best of it, or quit. A few brokers left. One went back to school for an MBA and some just took other jobs.

This is about the time I figured I needed to get tough. I put my head down and went to work harder than ever. I wanted to open 100 accounts in six months. I put everything else out of my mind and solely concentrated on opening accounts. I loved the Conseco (CNC at the time) story. Stephen Hilbert built up this insurance company from an initial $10,000 investment into one of the best-performing companies on the New York Stock Exchange throughout the 1990s. It was a sensational growth story, which made it easy to open accounts on. I was averaging one account a day. Our corner office turned into an account-opening machine. The junior brokers and cold callers would hand me leads all day and say, "This one is hot" or "He's ready to go." People would go from a name in a directory to a lead on an index card to either an account or the garbage can after three attempts to open the account.

In the weekly sales meetings the managers called me an anomaly and used me as an example, asking how many accounts I had opened so far that week or that month. I made it look easy, but it was mentally tough. From the time I came into the office to the time I left, including Saturdays, I pitched Conseco. I was in the Zone! On my best days, I would open four or five accounts. That was a real high. When asked how I did it, I would say I brainwashed myself. Opening accounts was all I thought about. There was a lot of mental preparation in getting ready to block out all distractions during each day, and believe me, there were tons of possible distractions. Our section of the office was loaded with young, action-seeking brokers. When the market would not provide any action, there would be the TV, blaring baseball games or horse races (one broker owned a race horse). Then there was the guys who loved to chitchat about the market, economy, interest rates, or anything else related to our business. Of course, there were always the lunch breaks that started out so innocently at the Rio-Grande (which has the strongest margaritas in New York City) and ended up lasting until sometime around midnight.

So to keep my head on straight, the process started in my morning shower. I would tell myself, "I am going to open at least one account today and most likely I'll open three. I will not get off the phone all day until I do. I have a job to do, and I'm going to be great at it." This would continue on the train ride in and in the elevator ride up to the office. Believe me, it worked, and it continues to work for people that know this principle: You need to zero in on exactly what you want, be precise, and focus intently on it to the point that you see it, feel it, and smell it. Be careful, though, because if you're not thorough in your vision, you may realize when you get it that it is not exactly what you had in mind. So think it through, imagine the outcome, and work out all the details ahead of time.

This may sound nuts, but it's like the magic genie–wish type of thing. If you ask for the wrong thing, wish for the wrong thing, or focus your time and energy on the wrong thing, it may be too late by the time you make it happen. This bit of advice should be sold for $200,000 just so people would realize the true worth of it, but it should also come with a bright yellow caution sticker.

During my account-opening stint, I wasn't making much money, because all I was doing was opening accounts. I was not working my book and hardly trading or re-positioning, which is the stuff that generates commissions. In turn, I was having a hard time paying my bills. The new mortgage, the BMW lease, and my credit card bills were strangling me. I kept telling myself that things would pick up and that when they did it would be worth it with all of the new accounts. And when things got even tougher, I figured I could pull some equity out of my house and make some money in the market. Bad idea; the $50,000 equity line was gone just like that. The market was terrible, and this was not the time to be trying to make money by trading.

It was around this time that I married my high school sweetheart, Lina. I remember we were on our honeymoon in Greece and I was wondering what else I could do in life. Greece was a great place to daydream. The pace there is slow as molasses. The beaches are out of this world—clear blue endless water meets the clear blue sky—and the heat makes everyone slow down about 50 percent. It's easy to become mesmerized as the warm breeze and the smell of sea salt hits your skin and relaxes your senses. On our visit, they had a heat wave; the temperature hit 118 degrees! We were walking up the little mountain to the Acropolis and feeling dizzy due to the heat. All the Greek tour guides were carrying umbrellas to block the sun. We stayed in the scorching city of Athens for two days, and then it was off to Santorini and then finally to the Island of Mikonos, the whole time surrounded by centuries-old beautiful homes and mountainside villages, all white with blue roofs. Through all of this I kept thinking about how to get out of the Wall Street rat race. Maybe open a bar, a restaurant, or sell medical supplies. I was dreaming of my escape, another life away from the daily grind and the fast-paced hustle and bustle of the Street. I guess its human nature to think that when things are great and the market is flying, there is no place in the world you would rather be, but when things turn bad, it is the place from which you most want to run. I would daydream about working outside, doing anything—construction or landscaping—as long as it kept my mind off declining stocks.

Once back home, I was still thinking about the open-air cafés in Greece, with people sitting around having coffee without a care in the world, or the restaurants where the dinner crowd starts at 9 p.m. and lingers until the wee hours. We had started out going to dinner at 6 p.m., and there were people still having lunch. Each day, we ate later and later until we finally got into the swing of the Euro late-night dinner thing. On our second to last night in Mikonos, our leisurely dinner started around 10 p.m. We lingered, having two bottles of wine with plates of feta cheese and olives, overlooking the harbor until nearly 3 a.m. We spoke about our dreams and ambitions and how happy we were to be finally married after years of dating, fighting, and breaking up, only to make up and get back together again. We watched the moon rise and then set over the Mediterranean Sea. We watched the cruise boats way out in the distance lit up under the full moon as they waited in line to make it into the small port to dock for the night. It was one of the most romantic nights of our honeymoon.

Within a month or so of returning home, Lina answered the phone. It was Bank of New York, requesting payment on the $50,000 equity line. The credit line was news to Lina. She took it well, though. She had faith that I would bounce back, although she was a little upset that I didn't tell her about the loan in the first place. After a few weeks of being back in the office, I got caught up in the daily grind and forgot the relaxation that swept over me in Greece.

This was a tough time for all transaction brokers. A transaction broker is a broker that makes the majority of their commission buying and selling stocks. The better the market, the more volatility, the more commission is generated through trading. I was working hard, but it was still a tough time because there was not a lot of money coming in. The brokers in the office would go on long lunches, hang around someone's office, and often end up at the bar by early afternoon. My thoughts were predominantly on paying my bills and just making a living.

One Sunday afternoon I was reading the Sunday *Times* going through the help wanted ads and can remember truly thinking about a career change. It was tough working so hard for such small rewards, especially when I started to wonder if what I was aiming for was really a light at the end of the tunnel or just an illusion. You see, it's easy to get revved up and excited about an idea for a day. Everyone does. Some even stay excited about an idea for a week, and a few may be able to stay worked up and excited for a month or more. I know, however, that a winner needs to stay excited for as long as it takes to win, keeping in mind the payoff at the end of the journey. There would be many chances to quit, many chances to walk away. But once my mind is made up, I stick with it till the end.

There are some people, and I am one of them, that really get revved up about things, such as an idea or a project. These people quite often have high highs and low lows. During the good times, there is no stopping us. We are invincible, never seeing the downside or the danger lurking just around the corner. Then when things turn and they get tough, it's a real fight to stay positive. This is when working out and meditation has pulled through for me.

My 99-year-old grandfather, who worked out for an hour a day up until a year ago, believes whole-heartedly that working out is the best thing you can do for yourself. He is a retired colonel from the air force and lives in Riverside, California. I try hard to take his advice. There is no doubt about it; working out and meditating helps you stay positive. This methodology can get you through even the toughest times. It releases certain chemicals into your bloodstream that are like happy particles that flow through your blood to your brain to cheer you up. These naturally manufactured chemicals are serotonin, adrenaline, and endorphins. By getting all three of these into your bloodstream at the same time, your spirit can soar to remarkable heights. To get the triple rush, as I call it, you need to work out for thirty to forty minutes and then meditate for another twenty to thirty minutes. This is the best time to read something stimulating, like inspirational biography, which motivates you to follow your dreams. When you feel really upset or blue, try this and see what happens.

After seven or eight months of opening accounts on Conseco, I had roughly 50,000 shares on the books and about 200 new accounts. The stock was trading at around \$40 a share. This is when things started to get real interesting.

Before we venture into this next cycle, let me give you a snapshot of my new family's financial situation. We were more than \$150,000 in debt, including the equity loan but not including the mortgage on the house. When the market collapsed, my account was not only wiped out, it went negative, meaning I owed the firm close to \$30,000. This is because of margin. What this means is that things came down so fast that before I could sell to cover a margin call, my account went negative. Making the payments to everyone on what I was bringing in was next to impossible. I had no choice but to work like crazy to open accounts in hopes of getting out from this mountain of debt. I had faith that things would pick up. Needless to say, bankruptcy was in the back of my mind. I tried to keep it there, but every now and then I was tempted to throw in the towel.

As Richard Dawkins writes in *The Selfish Gene,* "The rabbit runs faster than the fox, because the rabbit is running for his life while the fox is only running for his dinner." Right about here I was starting to feel like a rabbit.

Chapter Five
Here we go again

"The Internet is the Viagra of big business."
–Jack Welch, Chairman and CEO, General Electric

"The effect of these technologies could rival and arguably even surpass the impact the telegraph had prior to, and just after, the Civil War."
—Alan Greenspan, Chairman of the Board of Governors of the Federal Reserve System, U.S. News & World Report, *June 19, 2000*

All of the previous ups and downs, as dramatic as they were, turned out to be just a warm-up for what was about to explode and completely sweep me away, then unravel and knock my lights out. This time things were going to be different. (Whenever you hear these words, look out!) I had been reading dozens of trading books, such as:

- *Reminiscences of a Stock Operator* by Edwin Lefevre
- *Extraordinary Popular Delusions and the Madness of Crowds* by Charles Mackay
- *More Extraordinary Popular Delusions and the Madness of Crowds* by Joseph Bulgatz
- *Trade Your Way to Financial Freedom* by Van Tharp
- *Stock Market Logic* by Norman Fosback
- *The Market Wizards* by Jack Schwager
- *The New Market Wizards* by Jack Schwager
- *Pit Bull, Lessons from Wall Street's Champion Trader* by Martin Swartz

Armed with the knowledge from these books and dozens more, plus the training from Freddie Ballou on The Program, as he called it, I was able to handle things much better this time around. Now I used stop loss orders; I didn't put more than 10 percent of the account in any one position; I looked for stocks that fit a certain criteria, such as having good earnings and breaking out of a trading range; I paid close attention to volume, especially when there was a spike with no news; and I watched for unusual option activity or unusual premiums in the options. The 18-day rule was another trading technique, which is, simply, after 18 trading days of a new offering, the firm that brought them public will put a buy rating on the stock and you usually get a nice pop in the stock price. This happened almost all the time because of the quiet-period regulation. I would look for a stock that was bouncing off a double bottom or, even better, a triple bottom or, even better yet, bouncing off a triple bottom with over two or three times normal volume, on no news. These would give you a nice trade.

A double or triple bottom is when a stock bounces off a support level two or three times without falling below it. A trading range is simply the range a stock would trade between for a week or even a month. Let's say the stock trades between $10 and $14 per share for four weeks. Then all of a sudden it blows through $14 on large volume. This is usually a very good sign, and in good markets it should send the stock higher in the near term.

In 1998 the market started to really heat up and Internet stocks started exploding. My goal was to find a stock that was not discovered yet, such as a company that had an Internet component that was not priced into the market capitalization yet. I found one and got real excited about it: Data Broadcast (DBCC). They had a popular website called Marketwatch.com that they were going to spin off. Right before the spin-off of an Internet company that everyone wants to own, the parent company gets bid up big time. I dumped most of Conseco and plowed into DBCC. It was a good thing I was able to sell most of the shares, because Conseco ran into some problems and went into bankruptcy protection a few years later. Within a few months, DBCC flew from the single digits to the twenties, then thirties. Needless to say, my commissions for that month were huge. That was it; people thought I was a genius. My buddy Artie Buisson had originally brought DBCC to my attention but unfortunately did not load up on it like I did. Artie is now a trader on the floor of the NYSE.

The next idea may not have worked so well, but that was okay because I did not give it much room on the downside. I was using tight stop losses. I had created a lot of wealth for my accounts, and I wanted to protect it. I also knew that these assets would generate a ton of commissions. I had close to 100,000 shares of DBCC in my book, all under $16 to $18 per share, with some purchased as low as $7. This move gave my book new life. I was back!

The years 1998 and 1999 were an insane time to be a stockbroker! I mean a real stockbroker—those who made a living buying and selling stocks, as most of the brokers at Gruntal at the time did. Not bond brokers, financial planners, or insurance salesman, I mean honest-to-goodness stockbrokers. All the brokerage firms these days are trying their hardest to convert this group to become salesman of other products, like money managers or mutual funds. Real stockbrokers are becoming scarce, and with the Internet and the deep discount brokers, it will be hard for them to survive. This is an extremely challenging profession. I often heard from broker buddies how often they were just about ready to call it quits. Then it hits them: What else could I do? The answer to this question keeps most of them grounded. The ups and downs are almost unbearable, but the options may seem limited. That's because life as a stockbroker is a unique experience. When times are good, the money that can be earned is mind-boggling, but when things turn, it's like torture. It's often hard to switch careers to what would most likely be less exciting, more structured, and a reduction in earnings. Then there are also the lingering memories of the good old days and the hopes that they'll return. The memories of how much money can be made in a good market pulls them through the bear markets.

Like I was saying, the years 1998, 1999, and the beginning of 2000 are years that will be compared to the tulip mania in Holland throughout the 1620s, the South Sea Bubble in England from 1711 to 1720, and even the Roaring Twenties. It was a time that no stockbroker or investor will ever forget. They say an investment or speculative bubble comes along once in a generation, and this was ours!

The market had heated up so fast and out of nowhere that by the time we were halfway into it, we still did not fully realize what was going on. The commissions that brokers were earning exploded as prices rocketed upward. I went from doing under $10,000 a month to around $100,000 a month. My best month was around $180,000 in commission. After taxes and what I owed the firm (payment toward a negative balance in my margin account), I took home around $37,000 for that month. Lina applied the whole check to pay down our debt. This was my biggest month, and I didn't see a penny of it. I handed the check over, and that was the end of it.

I was totally absorbed by the market. I would do research on my home computer until almost midnight and then wake up in the morning and reach for the remote to see what the futures were doing. The pre-market trades would continuously go by on CNBC, and I'd be glued to the ticker. Then I would grab a cup of coffee and head to the computer to see once again where the stocks I was trading were in the pre-market and check for news. Because of the Internet, information had become more widely disseminated than in any other time in history. It was as if things were upside down. Twentysomething's were starting companies that were going to change the world, and they were raising millions—sometimes hundreds of millions, and some even valued in the billions. A good portion of these companies were losing money, with a few hundred million dollars' of market capitalization and no profits to show for itself. This was the first time in history that companies losing money were going public. And going public at a rapid-fire pace. But you had to see the big picture. As the pioneers and spokesman for the new digital economy would say, "You either get it or you don't."

I got it. I really did. I was a believer, especially because I was doing $5,000, $10,000, and sometimes even $20,000 a day in commissions because of these companies and the runaway market. It seemed like all a company had to do was add a "dot com" to their name and the stock would take off. The thinner the float—meaning the fewer shares available for purchase—the greater the news affected the share price. The market was valuing Internet companies based on the future.

The thought was that if you could create a niche, get people interested, and lure them to the website, you'll eventually figure out how to generate revenue from them. Everyone seemed to accept this as gospel and thus price the companies accordingly. The few naysayers would practically be stoned.

The main transformation of the world economy, via the Internet, had to do with the ability for information to be widely disseminated at light speed. There was no place a transformation of this magnitude would be felt more than the U.S. securities markets. Information is the pivotal point for action. There is no real action without information. Think of the Battle of Waterloo. Nathan Rothschild had an agent who, as soon as victory was certain, set off to London to inform Rothschild, who in turn loaded up on British government shares. He unloaded, at huge profits, as everyone else got the news. He acted on information.

Truly insightful entrepreneurs who are bright enough to understand what is happening and act swiftly have the ability to make a fortune. TokyoJoe is an excellent case in point. Because of this stock trader's clever wit, outspoken manner, and stock-picking ability, he created a following from chat rooms and message-board crowds. He then started the website Tokyojoe.com and charges an arm and a leg for membership. His mere mention of a stock would increase the volume exponentially and send the price substantially higher.

In my office I had four phone lines and a cell phone. At least two lines were going at all times during market hours, and sometimes I would have a phone on each ear. My junior broker, Anthony, a sixtyish-year-old ex–Wall Street wire operator who was laid off from Shearson in a downsizing, could barely keep up. He would help my assistant, Lisa, answer the phones and give people quotes all day. Some of the new accounts I had opened during my account-opening spree turned out to be super-active accounts when the market heated up. Two in particular were Morris and Rahul. They alone would keep Anthony on the phone all day long. Anthony would go from one to the other entering orders nonstop. Clients would wait on hold for as long as fifteen minutes to ask my opinion on a stock or to put in an order. My office was like Grand Central Station, with phone lights blinking all day, CNBC on the TV, the squawk box blaring in the background, and faxes and mail being dropped on my desk. Then there were the other brokers in the office, running around full of enthusiasm with a tale or two of the next big trade. You would hear a roar when a particular stock the office was trading had a big move. At the end of the day, I would count the pages of orders entered. There would be eight or ten trades on each page. By this time, we had on-line order entry, where you could enter the orders from your computer. Some days I would have more than twenty pages of orders. It would take me an hour just to give them a quick check to make sure there were no mistakes.

Most days I would grab a few beers for the train ride home to help me unwind. On the extremely wild days, I would head to our office's bar of choice—Saga on Lexington Avenue, located around the corner. There would always be a group of brokers from our office there having a few drinks. Whenever one of us would walk in, the rest of the brokers would cheer and the bartenders would change the TV station to CNBC so we would feel right at home.

When the market was really moving, it would be tough to keep track of everything, and every now and then there was a mistake. One broker, who meant to buy 10,000 shares of some stock, sold it instead. The error generated a $100,000 loss by the time he found it a few hours later. The firm let him pay it off over two years. Whenever anything really good or really bad happened, it circulated through the office like wildfire. If John LaBarka, a broker and buddy who sat in the office next to mine, traded the same stock as I did and it started to move, we would bang on the wall so hard we thought it would collapse. If it was a real move, say 5 to 10 points, my whole side of the office would start banging on the walls. The cheering and moaning that went along with the rises and dips in the market was like being at some crazy sporting event. Everyone always knew what everyone else was trading, and when someone got clobbered, everyone knew about it.

At Gruntal the top producers were treated well, as with most of the larger firms. Each month one of the managers, Al Palladino, would take the top five producers to the Sky Club on the 56th floor of 200 Park Avenue. This posh members-only club was directly across the street from our office. The Third Avenue branch had moved to 777 Lexington Avenue, on the corner of Lexington and 42nd Street. The building had two addresses. Being on the corner, the other address was 150 East 42nd Street—the old Mobile headquarters. Everything in the Sky Club is dark wood and brown leather. The chairs seemed to have extra cushion and were ultra-comfortable. It was at one of these meetings that Al told us about some type of business-club meeting in which both he and Donald Trump were members. I remember him telling me about having listened to Donald talk about his future plans and thinking he was nuts because his ideas were so inconceivable. This was before Donald became The Donald. I was very interested and wanted to drill him on the subject, but being the aspiring stockbroker, I resisted the urge to linger on the topic once the conversation returned to the business at hand. Besides these extra perks in the city, the top producers were awarded annual trips similar to PaineWebber's. One such all-expense-paid extravaganza was to Amelia Island in Florida. Lina and I had an unforgettable time. In the morning the brokers would attend a presentation of some sort while the spouses would enjoy a massage or just lounge around in the sun. The rest of the day was spent sailing, golfing, tennis, swimming, dining and networking.

In the meantime, my trading system was working out fabulously. Most of the other brokers would ask me to explain "The Program" to them. I was earning huge commissions, while the values of my customer accounts were increasing as well. It truly felt great, and I was glad to be paying down my debt from the last time around. It seems like each cycle got more vicious. The ups were greater and the downs more severe. These swings were amplified by me having more on the line each time with more accounts, larger accounts, and more money in my personal account.

After the 1997 wipeout, when my account went negative, my manager asked me to close my account and concentrate on building my business, which I did for a while. Once it was paid off and the slate was cleaned, there was no stopping me from opening it back up and letting it rip all over again—especially when the market caught fire and stocks that were all coiled up ready for a moon shot were exploding through their old highs like a blow torch through blotting paper. A company would be mentioned during CNBC's power lunch, and I would own a thousand shares before they could finish their sentence and then have sold before the commercial break. Everyone had a tip, and everyone wanted to get a tip. If a stock had anything to do with the Internet or broke out of a lengthy trading range, it could move as much as 50 percent in a week or so. It was a wild time. The volatility and the valuations were unprecedented and could send even the coolest-mannered trader home at the end of the day with the shakes.

When I called Arty, who was trading on the floor of the NYSE, and told him I was writing a book about the ups and downs of Wall Street in the '90s, he replied that he had the shakes all over again from just thinking about the craziness of 1999.

One day I turned to my buddy, Joe, and said, "Remember these times, Joe. You only go through this once in a lifetime." He still remembers that comment and is sort of spooked by it. It's hard to step back or step outside of a world that is so all-consuming. While going through it, it's hard to imagine anything different. I think the ability to remove oneself from the emotion of the moment is what separated the ordinary trader from the supertraders or even the geniuses. Believe me, it's next to impossible to ignore stocks as they go from 3 to 75 in a month, especially when it happens over and over. It was easy to get completely swept away. Everywhere you went, CNBC was on the TV, including the bars, restaurants, and barber shops, and the reporters made the market into a big game. CNBC had a half-time show midway through the trading day. The market became the new American pastime; everyone had an opinion and a story. At every party or social gathering, people would love to chat about their stocks and how much they were making and what the next big winner was going to be.

With the market devouring all my time, I hardly had time to focus on family life. Fortunately, Lina was very understanding and patient and was always great about planning our vacations. If it weren't for her persistence, we wouldn't have had too many trips outside the ones provided by the firms. But for all the many wonderful adventures she planned, the trips to Italy to visit her family were by far the most enjoyable.

On one such occasion, we flew into Rome and stayed there for three days. We stayed in a five-star hotel a few blocks from the Spanish

Steps in the center of the city. It was a summer trip, so Rome was warm day and night. I remember walking around and splashing my head in the fountains, including the Fontana Di Trevi. Lina could not get me out of the Sistine Chapel. We were in there for close to six hours. We got lost in the beauty and grandeur of the Vatican City. The sheer opulence, combined with knowing that its history dates back to antiquity and that people have been coming to the Vatican for almost two thousand years to pray over the tombs of the apostle Peter and more recent pontiffs, is almost too much to comprehend. Taking in the artwork and sculptures of the most famous artists in history can have a tremendously uplifting and inspirational effect. From Bernini to Michelangelo and Maderno, when you leave there, you take something more than just a memory.

The cafés in Greece were great, but the restaurants, cafés and trattorias in Rome were superb. It's something about the atmosphere and history in the surrounding buildings that just makes it feel as though it is a different time and place. The buildings are constructed with impressive stonework, and the inside of the bars and restaurants are overflowing with details. The roads and sidewalks are mostly cobblestone and brick, which adds to the beauty and ancient charm. Sitting in the cafés having an espresso and a panini or a pizza and a birra is truly unforgettable.

While in our hotel room in Rome, I would log on to the Internet and check stock prices. They were really moving right along, to borrow a phrase from Maggie Mahar, author of *Bull! (A History of the Boom 1982–1999:* "IPO's were popping like champagne corks."

After three days in Rome, we headed to the Abruzzi region, about two hours west. We took a local train and were met at the station by Lina's cousin Mossimo. They owned the most exclusive restaurant in Sulmona and resided above it. Our room had mountain views and a mural on the ceiling. Her grandfather, nonno Corradino, lives there as well. The days flew by. We did a lot of visiting, a lot of eating, and a fair amount of sightseeing. The center of the city was only a few blocks away. Her nonno would walk there daily to play cards, pick up the daily newspaper, and have espresso.

My brother- and sister-in-law, Anna and Joe DelPozzo, were there as well. They were staying on the other side of Sulmona with another one of Lina's aunts, Zia Adriana.

Sunday was great. The whole day was about getting ready for dinner. Joe and I ventured into town with Lina's uncle, Zio Celestino. First we went to the fish store, then to the butcher, was and, finally, to the cheese store and bakery. Everything had to be fresh. I was starving by the time we ate, at around two p.m., but after our ten-course meal, I could not see straight. We had dinner in the family restaurant downstairs, Ristorante Rigoletto. The walls are solid mahogany and the bar is marble. It really is like something in the movies. We can't wait until her cousins start getting married so we can go back!

Chapter Six
What Goes Up . . .

"The way to love anything is to realize that it may be lost."
– G. K. Chesterton, author

As this go-round was at its zenith, my 26-year-old sister-in-law, Anna DelPozzo, was admitted to the hospital for lupus-related complications with her pregnancy. After several traumatizing weeks of tests and many different explanations for what was happening, the doctors suggested she be induced. Joseph junior was delivered on February 13, 2000, and died in his father's hands in front of me two days later, on February 15, at Columbia Presbyterian Hospital in New York City. He was all of 1.10 lbs. He was a fighter until the very end, kicking and wriggling his arms while struggling to breathe. They said his organs weren't developed enough for him to survive.

At the same time, Anna was fighting for her own life. While trying to keep her spirits up, we were seeking answers from doctors and nurses. The story was never the same. They told us her platelet level in her blood dropped so low they needed to give her bags of platelets. At one point, they made a mistake and told us her platelet count rose to 70,000 or so from around 1,000. We were ecstatic, only to find out later they made a mistake due to a mix-up with test results. There had been no improvements in her platelet count at all. Less than two weeks later, Anna lost her fight against lupus. This was an unbearably painful few months for our family. It was like walking through a thick fog, being led actually, or pushed, because the numbness overtook your comprehension of what had actually transpired. Lina's parents, who lost their youngest daughter; my wife, Lina, who lost her only sibling; and Joe, who lost his wife and son, could barely grapple with the events that had taken place over the previous few weeks. My heart goes out to

Joe, and each night when I say prayers before bed with my two boys, Codi and Luca, we pray for his family and their cousin.

To keep their memory alive and to raise money to find a cure for lupus, Lina, Joe and I, along with a small board of close friends, started an annual fundraiser, which over the last three years raised more than $100,000 for the Anna and Joseph DelPozzo, Jr., Lupus Memorial Fund. (Feel free to e-mail me at **LupusMemorial@Delkingmgt.com** if you would like more information.) We hold an annual dinner event at Luca's of Greenwich Connecticut, who does a great job every year.

Just when I was thinking life couldn't get much worse, the Mt. Everest–like peak of the NASDAQ fell apart—a 10-point drop in one stock and a 20-point drop in another. I knew it was going to happen sooner or later. It was just too easy to make so much money. Even so, most people were like deer staring into the headlights, saying things like, "Things will stabilize soon" or "I'll lighten up on the bounce," but the bounce never came. Some of the really margined accounts were dropping as much as 25 percent in a week. It is truly unbelievable how the mood on Wall Street can change so swiftly.

A strategy that I came up with during the Internet blast-off was to use option premium to create buying power. It went something like this:

Let's say XYZ stock is trading at $52.
Buy 1,000 shares of XYZ stock at $52.
Sell 10 XYZ calls (leaps) for $30 with a strike price of $55.

This means you are selling the right for someone to buy XYZ from you at $55 sometime in the future. The purchaser of the calls is paying you $30.

There are two components that make up the price of an option, either a call or a put. One component is the intrinsic value. That is the amount of the option that is in the money, or the portion that is over the strike price. With the above example, the strike price is $55 and the price of the stock is $52, so there is no intrinsic value. If, on the other hand, the price of the underlying stock is $60, the intrinsic value would be $5. The rest of the price of the option is called time premium, or the time value. This is the portion that decreases over time. The time value is also known as the premium. The premium is the component of the option that increases with volatility.

When you sell a covered call, the amount of the call that is out of the money—that is, over the strike price (or the premium)—hits the account and creates two times that amount as buying power. With the above example, it means that if you were able to sell the call at $30, you would have two times that amount as buying power. This also means you would have $60 in buying power and the stock would cost $52. With this example, you would have an additional $8 in buying power, or $8,000 (if based on 1,000 shares).

Another way is to look at this as reducing your cost to 52 – 30 = 22 and agree to sell at $55. At the time the option expires, if the stock price is over the strike price of $55, the purchaser of the option has the right to buy the stock at $55 from the seller.

These are hypothetical examples, and the actual premiums may be much less. Remember, this was during a huge financial bubble, when many things were out of whack and premiums were unusually high due to above average volatility. Different clearing firms may have different margin requirements, so the above examples may differ on the amount of buying power they create. Also, more volatile stocks, such as those of Internet companies, may not be fully marginable—or marginable at all—with some clearing firms.

The net effect on the account, depending on the margin requirements at the firm, would be to create both equity and buying power. Although it is not liquid equity, it is equity that you can use for buying power nonetheless. This buying power can work two ways if you choose to use it. You can make money with it, or you can lose money with it. The problem is, if you lose money, with this manufactured buying power, the account can go to a negative liquidation value. This means that if you were forced to liquidate, the account would be negative. If you think about this, it could create a never-ending cycle. You can create buying power and buy stock with it, then create more buying power and buy more stock with that buying power. The problem is, when the market completely falls apart or has a violent drop, it can bring a leveraged account to zero and lower very quickly.

Over time, the option premium decreases. (The premium is the portion of the option known as the time value.) As time goes by, this time-value portion of the option goes down. Let's say you sell someone the right, or an option, to buy an apple two years in the future for $2.40 over what the apple is worth. Theoretically, every month over the next two years, the premium portion of the contract value should decrease by $0.10. As this happens, the person who sells the option makes $0.10 a month. Well, it would be the same with Apple Computer. If you sell the option or right to buy the stock from you two years in the future, people will pay a time premium over what it is worth at the moment in hopes that the stock will move up. People pay this time premium because they are betting that during the two years, the stock will rise above the strike price and therefore be greater than the amount of premium they are paying. Even if it is, the premium portion of the option contract still decreases.

As this premium decreases, the liquidation value of the account increases for the account that has sold the options, thus creating real liquid equity. I did create a complex tangled account that was hard for most people to comprehend. It was very risky and very volatile. On a large scale, I did this only in my own account. With the market rising as it was, the premiums on the active stocks went through the roof. I used Telescan to search every day for unusual premiums in the option market. The larger premiums allowed you to create more buying power and more equity when you wrapped one up. That is, when you bought the stock and sold the call option.

This strategy, through using leverage, increases the volatility in an account tremendously. So with such a leveraged account, combined with a market where the bottom fell out, I experienced accounts dropping faster than I would ever imagine. The new millennium hit me like a punch right in the nose and then another one right behind it. I was wiped out all over again, but this time I really felt like the rug was pulled right out from under me, hurling me right onto my head. I had finally reached my goal of doing a million dollars in commission in 1999, only to be completely cleaned out in 2000. As you can see from

The severity of the decline in the chart below, tech stocks were falling and falling fast. I did my best to protect my clients, but it was hard to salvage the aggressive accounts. I had lost all of my personal money—again—and had no real desire or fight left in me to go through another cycle.

I thought long and hard about rebuilding the business but didn't have the energy for it this time around. My boundless passion for the business was completely gone. I needed a change. The loss in the NASDAQ was so brutal, it lost more than 70 percent over the next two years, and most of the Internet companies were either out of business or down more than 90 percent. It was truly crunch time.

Below, a chart provided by www.economagic.com of the NASDAQ Composite from 1999–2001.

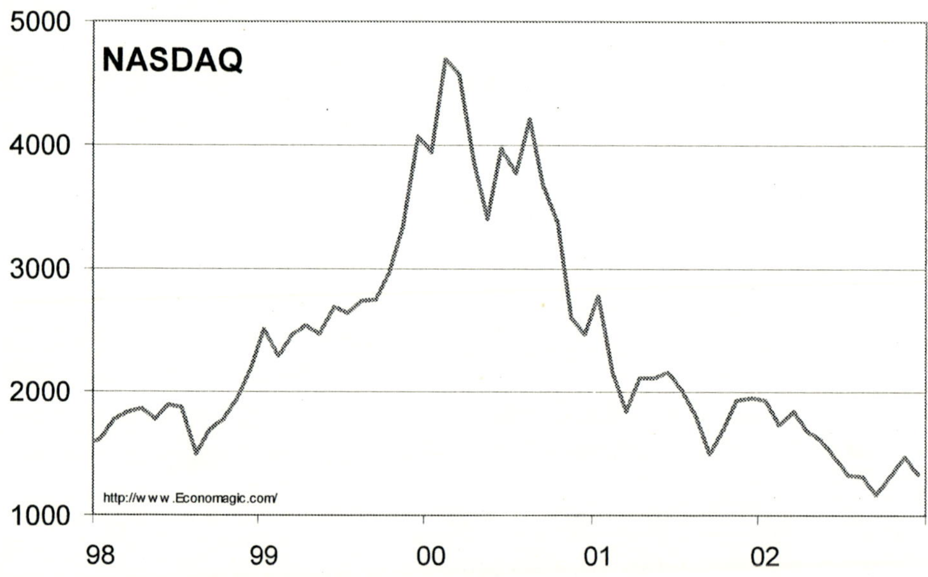

Below, the NASDAQ Composite from when I entered the business in April of 1990 until I left the business in 2001.

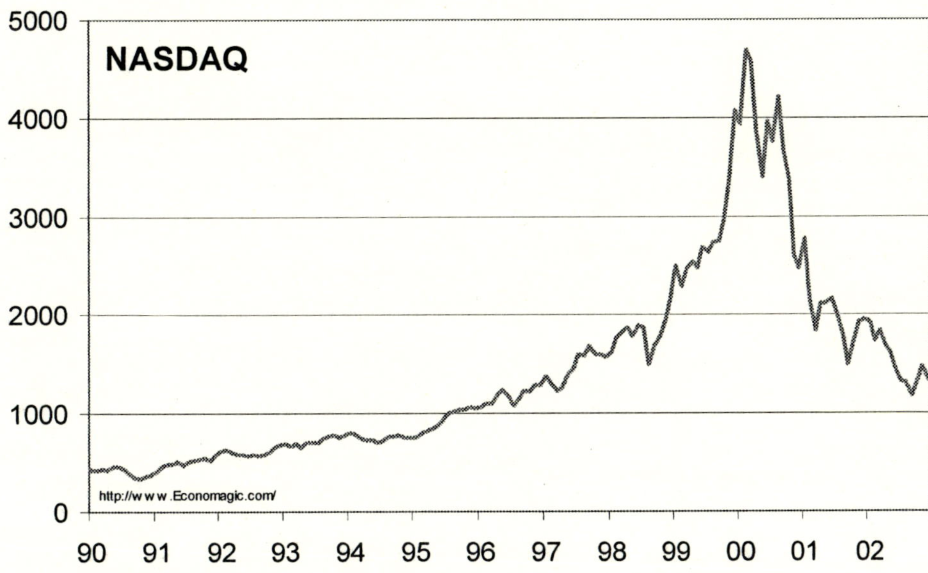

PART II

Chapter Seven
Buying Our First Two Properties

"Far better it is to dare mighty things, to win glorious triumphs even though checkered by failure, than to rank with those poor spirits who neither enjoy nor suffer much because they live in the gray twilight that knows neither victory nor defeat."
– President Theodore Roosevelt

It's clear that I was spinning my wheels as a stockbroker. It was like running on one of those wheels they put in cages for animals to run on, just to burn energy and never get anyplace, or like a dog chasing its tail. I say this now, looking back with 20/20 vision, but I believed quite the opposite at the time. I believed then that I was building a business for myself. A business that I would run the way I saw fit. A business I put together piece by piece, client by client, account by account. It was a sort of business, but then again it was more of a job. My book of clients was mine, as long as I stayed at the firm and as long as I did what the firm told me. As soon as I left, however, my book was distributed to the other brokers, who did their best to keep those clients as their own.

A real wake-up call came after a fellow broker passed away. Only in his late thirties, he had worked diligently for more than ten years at the firm and was bringing in somewhere north of $500,000 in commissions a year. He went home one day, said hello to his wife and two sons, said his chest hurt, went upstairs to lie down before dinner, and never got back up. He had a heart attack. The next day, his book was handed out to a select few brokers. A book he spent years building. To be fair, there was some talk about setting aside a portion of the commissions from his clients for his wife, but I am not sure to what extent this happened. I hope he was well insured.

The point, for me, was clear: This book of clients was not really mine. Ultimately, the firm would decide its fate if something were to happen to me. There are plenty of other jobs where you don't "build something," like regular salaried jobs. Life insurance is one protection for people who are not building something, in the form of a lasting business, for their family. Life insurance acts as a safety net for the family if the breadwinner suddenly passes away.

The way I was beginning to see it was that if I were going to put all my energy into building a business, like I did in the brokerage business, I want it to be truly, indisputably, my business. Life is too short. If I'm going to crank out twelve-hour days, I want to make sure I create something of permanent value.

This brings me to my buddy Scott Jerutis. He was fed up with the business a bit before me and was looking for an exit as well. Sometime in 1999 he purchased an eleven-unit apartment complex for roughly $650,000. Of this, he put down approximately $130,000. The property created an initial monthly cash flow of roughly $2,800. However, the rents were below market and he was able to raise them. The increase in rents brought his monthly cash flow to over $4,000. During this time, he was losing all interest in the business. I don't think he was doing any real commissions to speak of, and he wasn't a big believer in the Internet bubble; therefore, he did not often trade technology stocks. He did do a stint downtown, in the Wall Street office at the institutional desk, but I think his heart was in real estate. Even so, he still couldn't bring himself to fully let go and call it quits.

I remember questioning him repeatedly about his real estate purchase, going over the details step by step. The cash-flow concept was blowing me away. I was fascinated that he had created a stream of cash flow that would come in every month without him having to deal with the brokerage business anymore. Probably several dozen times I would call him up and say, "Okay, let's start from the top. You put down $130,000." He would stop me and say no, because I got a credit for the current month rents and the security deposits at closing, so the amount was closer to $115,000.

At this time, I began reading Robert Kiyosaki's *Rich Dad Poor Dad,* which is one of the best real estate books I've ever encountered. I highly recommend it as a great starting point. Upon finishing it, the real estate seed was planted. Thereafter, all I read were real estate biographies: The Reichmanns, Donald Trump, Fred French, John Jacob Astor, Robert Campou, Bill Zeckendorf, and Trammell Crow. I was, and still am, enthralled and enthused by these empire builders. I wanted to know everything I could about them. How they thought, how they started, what techniques they used, and, most important, how they fared.

Again and again I would ask Scott to repeat the story from the beginning in case I missed something. From your original $115,000, I would repeat, you now have a monthly cash flow of $3,000 or $4,000, just like that. He would explain that it took a lot of searching, a lot of looking at deals, and a lot of number crunching. He also had the foresight to know that he would be able to raise the rents, therefore increasing the value of the building.

For example, he would explain that if I raise the rents $100 per unit x 11 units, this would generate an extra $1,100 per month. Multiplying that by 12 equals an extra $13,200 a year. He was actually able to raise rents more than that, but let's imagine that he was able to go up $200 a month per unit:

$200 per unit = $2,200 a month = $26,400 a year

This makes the property more valuable. For a simple rule of thumb, let's argue that an additional $26,400 to the net income would add ten times that to the value of the property.

Around this time, properties were trading at roughly ten times their net income. So by increasing rents $200 a unit per month, the value of the property increased roughly $264,000 over the course of a year.

This really got my full attention! Still in disbelief, I would repeat, "Scott, you put $115,000 down to buy the property, raised rents, and are now making over $40,000 a year? In addition, you were able to pull your original $115,000 out, along with an additional $200,000, through the appreciation from refinancing?" He would reply, "Yes. Isn't it amazing?"

This was almost too much for me to conceive. We would kill ourselves in the brokerage business for this type of money and then have to do it all over again the next year because, as a stockbroker, you start out with zero commissions at the beginning of each month. I shared this information with my best friend since second grade, Denio, a remarkably talented builder, carpenter, and craftsman who worked in his family business, The DeLaurentis Bros. Construction Co. Because of his great skill and the fact that he is extremely dedicated, I believed he would be an excellent person to partner up with. So we decided to combine our talents and hunt for a deal. The only problem was, we had no money. Denio had been working for his father for the thirteen years while I was on Wall Street and neither of us had much liquid cash.

Throughout the late 1980s The DeLaurentis Bros. Construction Co. had grown to a multimillion-dollar enterprise, with hundreds of acres of land on which they constructed houses, one after the other. When it was time to put the roof on each property, they would have a "topping off" party. Everyone involved would show up—their accountant, the lawyers, and all the workers and family members who were in the business. However, when the housing market slowed in the early '90s, they were just about thrown into bankruptcy because the majority of their profit and cash flow came from selling newly constructed homes and they had overleveraged themselves. They were forced to sell all their land at giveaway prices and refinance everything they could, including their residences.

For several years thereafter, house sales practically slowed to a standstill, and The DeLaurentis Bros. Construction Co. had to take on smaller renovation jobs just to keep money coming in, which nearly all went into paying down their debt.

So Denio and I looked to each other for support. We began looking for deals in the paper, on the Internet, and anyplace else we could possibly think of. After about a week or two of coming up empty, we called Scott for inspiration. He said, "Come on, guys. Didn't you find a DEEEAAAL yet?" The problem was, none of them made sense. We wanted to mimic his deal, but we could not find one with that type of return. His starting-out return was close to 26 percent cash on cash, or a 12 percent cap rate, which means that if he had paid cash for the entire deal, he would net 12 percent, and with a mortgage, the return on the portion of the money he put down would be 26 percent. Notice the difference between the all-cash return and the "leveraged" return.

To get the money for our first deal, we refinanced our homes. We were both able to pull out roughly $80,000. This gave us about $160,000 to work with. We thought if we could find a deal like Scott's, earning 26 percent, we would pull out $1,700 each a month. This would be for starters. Then we would do improvements and raise rents. Both Denio and I knew firsthand the dangers of using leverage incorrectly, so we were determined to make sure our deals had cash flow for protection.

We set out again on our hunt and stumbled upon a place up in Pine Plains, New York, called Milanos, which had three bars, one of which was housed in a 5,000-square-foot atrium, along with a restaurant and pizza place. We loved the idea, because we both love to kick back and have nice long lunches. But when the reality of it set in, like the long hours and the workload, we decided against it.

We had agreed that the most important thing was the cash flow. Finally, after six months of looking at deals to no avail, I was ready to throw in the towel. Then, in April of 2001, Den found a building in the *Poughkeepsie Journal* that was advertised with a 28 percent return. The deal went like this:

Asking price:	$435,000
Gross income:	$ 95,000
Net income:	$ 58,000
Cap rate:	13.33%

It was a mixed-use building with roughly 8,000 square feet of office space and four apartments. It was Den that pushed us to drive up to Poughkeepsie to take a look. That's the beauty of a good partnership; one pushes the other when needed. The owner was a retired lieutenant colonel in the navy who had kept the building in neat and orderly condition. We offered him $400,000 on the spot. He requested that we put the offer in writing, which we did that very night, and the next day he accepted.

This is what the purchase-price snapshot looked like:

Purchase price: $400,000
Gross income: $ 95,000
Net income: $ 58,000
Cap rate: 14.50%

Down payment: $100,000 + $5,000 (closing cost) = $105,000

Net after mortgage: $30,000
Cash-on-cash return: 28.57%

We had our first accepted offer. It was exciting. For the $100,000 we would put up, we believed we would earn close to $30,000 a year, or 30 percent. This equaled about $1,250 each a month for the two of us. The closing was easy as pie. We got a loan with an 8 percent interest rate that would amortize over twenty-five years, with a five-year term. The loan was for $300,000, and we put $100,000 plus some closing costs down. Putting 25 percent down on a commercial deal is standard, although you can close deals with much less.

Every Saturday we made the one-hour drive to the property to paint and do other improvements. I remember standing in the parking lot looking at the building and feeling so proud that we owned it. That was a great feeling!

After deducting the down payment and all closing costs from our original $160,000, we had roughly $55,000 left from the refinance of our homes. While going through the waiting period to close on the first deal, the owner informed us that he had another, eighteen-unit brick apartment building he was selling right around the corner. He wanted $575,000 for it, or just under $32,000 a unit. We offered $500,000, but he would not come down in price. Without hesitation we agreed to the $575,000 asking price because we did not want to lose the deal. After spending six months looking for deals that had the cash flow to fit our criteria, we knew exactly what we wanted.

Once again, the problem was the down payment. The bank we had used for the first deal required 25 percent. This would be $575,000 x 25% = $143,750, plus closing costs of another $10,000 or thereabouts. Some of the closing costs can be bundled in with the mortgage. The only thing that came to mind was the remaining equity in our homes. Both Den and I were able to pull out another $93,000 in the form of an equity line of credit. This would give us another $186,000. All told, we had another $241,000 to spend on deals.

The 18-unit building looked like this:

Asking price: $575,000
Gross income: $122,100
Net income: $ 79,819
Cap rate: 13.88%

Down payment: $143,750 + $10,000 (closing cost) = $153,750

Net after mortgage: $40,696
Cash-on-cash return: 26.46%

With our second accepted offer, things were looking up. We were on a roll. We spent more time driving up to Poughkeepsie, looking into other deals, and just enjoying the fact that we were building something for ourselves and our families. The cash-flow concept was really starting to sink in. "Create cash flow" was our motto! We were not even taking into account the other aspects of owning real estate that are equally as important, if not more so. Like the equity we were building, both through principal paydown on the mortgage and appreciation. There are two types of appreciation. There is the regular, sit-back-and-do-nothing appreciation that happens with inflation, and there is forced appreciation. This occurs as you improve the property. You can improve a property in many ways, such as painting, putting pictures in the hallways, landscaping, remodeling kitchens and bathrooms, and upgrading tenants (meaning getting rid of noisy, troublemaking tenants who disturb others in the building). These improvements, in turn, add to higher rents. Maybe not right away, but by doing improvements you should be able to raise rents over time. You also improve a property's value by reducing expenses. For example: making sure no water is being wasted by leaking pipes or faucets, insulating windows and doors to help keep heat in during the winter, replacing older boilers with energy-efficient ones and shopping around for a good insurance rate. There are programs that even pay to have old, inefficient boilers replaced if you have lower-income tenants in a building. All these things—improvements to the building and cutting the expenses—increase the net income. The value of the building is for the most part determined by the net income, so by increasing the net income, you force appreciation.

Just think of the cash flow from these two buildings and the potentially long-lasting implications. Let's say we were taking in $1,200 each from the first building and $1,695 each from the second building. That's $2,895 each per month. This comes to $144 a day during a five-day workweek, just for waking up. Having spent time working on these buildings to improve them will lead to increasing the rents and additional cash flow each month.

The more we thought about this concept, the more excited we became. Now, $144 a day is not exactly hitting the jackpot, but for some people it takes a hard day's work to make that. Remember, I did not get to appreciation or principal paydown yet. These two things increase the overall return nicely. So, this $2,895 a month could conceivably add to our families' income indefinitely. Sure, there will be some issues to deal with—decisions to be made, repairs to be done, mortgages, bills, and other expenses to pay, and even the issue of having vacancies. On the other hand, we have gone months and even years at a time without a peep from these buildings except the monthly rents in the mail. Over time, with inflation, the rents have gone up considerably. This type of leverage is important to emphasize.

Lets say, as an example, that everyone in the eighteen-unit building was paying $565 each a month for rent, which adds up to $10, 175. If we were to raise the rent $50 per month each, that would come to an additional 8.8 percent.

The 18-unit building after $50 rent raise:

Asking price: $575,000
Gross income: $132,900
Net income: $ 90,619
Cap rate: 15.75%

Down payment: $143,750 + $10,000 (closing cost) = $153,750

Net after mortgage: $51,496 (up from $40,696)
Cash-on-cash return: 33.49% (up from 26.46%)

Just for this example, let's also assume that the expenses did not increase. (They do increase, of course, but I just want to illustrate the impact of leverage.) This 8.8 percent increase in the rent-roll extrapolates into a $10,800 a year increase in cash flow.

Or, as Den would inevitably ask, "How much more is that a month for us?" The monthly cash flow would go from $1,695 each to $2,145 each on this building. The effects of leverage will be even more profound when we look at appreciation.

In most of the apartments, there was ample room for upgrades and improvements. We would rip out the kitchens and bathrooms and replace them with everything new from Home Depot. In those instances, we were able to raise the rent as much as $300 a unit. Continuing with our example of the eighteen-unit building, let's say we redid four apartments a year and were able to raise the rents $200 each a month. That's an additional $800 a month, or $10,600 a year.

After Repairs:

Asking price: $575,000
Gross income: $143,500
Net income: $101,210
Cap rate: 17.6%

Down payment: $143,750 + $10,000 (closing cost) = $153,750

Net after mortgage: $62,077 (up from $40,696)
Cash-on-cash return: 40.37% (up from 26.46% originally)

There are a few ways to look at the cost of improvements. On average, they would be under $2,000 per apartment in materials and labor. In the beginning, we—mostly Den—did all the work. This is where his expertise really kicked in! As time went on, we hired workers to help with the improvements. With this example, let's add the cost of the improvements to the down payment to get a true picture of the return. At $2,000 a unit, doing four units, that's $8,000, bringing the $153,750 down payment to $161,750 for a total return on invested capital of 38.37 percent. We would pay for the materials out of the cash flow over time, never carrying any real credit card balance.

We were on the lookout for similar deals. The basic criteria was:

- Over a 13% cap rate
- Over 24% cash-on-cash return
- Room to raise rents, both because of being under market and by doing improvements

Over time the cap-rate portion of the criteria came down, as cap rates in general declined, but we tried to keep the cash-on-cash return up there. The improvements were a big factor. Denio, being a highly skilled builder and very handy with carpentry and woodwork, would prove invaluable as far as knowing how to save money on repairs and improve the buildings without breaking the bank. Our different strengths complemented each other well. The cash-flow concept had not only taken root in our brains, it had now forced us to branch out.

Chapter Eight
Our Third and Fourth Properties

"When you can't decide which of two evenly balanced courses of action to take, choose the bolder."

—*General W. J. Slim of the British army*

While driving around Poughkeepsie to find a place to have lunch, we found our next two deals. One was a blue wooden structure on a corner lot that housed several apartments, three buildings up from our first purchase. This one was on the market for a while, so we thought something must be wrong with it. When we called to find out how much they wanted and the particulars of the deal, the Realtor informed us that it was under contract. We pushed for more information, like the asking price and number of units. The seller wanted $165,000 for the six-unit building, or $27,500 per unit. We felt the price was a little high and being that it was supposedly under contract we decided to turn our attention elsewhere. Then we noticed a commercial building with a big red FOR SALE BY OWNER sign posted to its side. It was a stone-block building, roughly 24,000 square feet, on a corner right in the center of the town of Poughkeepsie. It had a combination of tenants, including a gym, karate dojo, an Italian delicacy distributor, and 13 office suites upstairs. This building had been on the market for nearly two years. We figured something must be wrong with this one as well. It looked a little neglected and was in need of a paint job and other minor improvements. However, it was completely occupied and had great cash flow. We met with the owner, Marty Sheer, who had actually built the building with his father in the 1950s. Over the years, various stores and businesses took up tenancy in the building, and one of his businesses—a travel agency—occupied space on the top floor.

These are the numbers based on the asking price:

Asking price: $300,000
Gross income: $ 85,800
Net income: $ 42,000
Cap rate: 14%

Down payment: $50,000 + $5,000 (closing cost) = $55,000

Net after mortgage: $18,744
Cash-on-cash return: 34%

We figured that with the building being on the market for so long and the fact that it seemed neglected; we had some room to negotiate. We offered $200,000, and Marty countered with $225,000, with him keeping his office there rent-free for two years. We accepted with the caveat that his secretary and bookkeeper, Lil, help us out for a few hours a week as needed. We had a deal. So not only were we buying an income property with nice cash flow, we were getting a part-time assistant. The office across from Marty's opened up just as we were closing on the deal, so we decided to use this space as our home base so we could be close to our other properties. Best of all, we had a gym, called East Coast Gym, right downstairs. Oddly enough, this was the name of the gym in Yonkers, New York which Den and I had belonged during high school. Before closing, we did a final inspection of the building and noticed some additional structural problems, so we lowered our bid to $218,000 to cover the cost of these repairs. Marty agreed, and we shook on the deal.

Here is a look at the numbers based on the purchase price:

Asking price: $218,000
Gross income: $ 85,800
Net income: $ 42,000
Cap rate: 19.26%

Down payment: $50,000 + $5,000 (closing cost) = $55,000

Net after mortgage: $26,190
Cash-on-cash return: 47.61%

Over the following three years, we were able to do several improvements, which in turn increased the rent. We installed hardwood floors in some of the units, painted the hallways and offices, and put in decorative molding and framed artwork throughout the building. Then we employed a strategy I learned from the various books I had read on billionaire New York real estate investor Harry Helmsley, who had built up his empire to more than $5 billion before his death in 1997. One of his tactics was to grieve the taxes as soon as he purchased a property. By arguing that the assessed value on the property (the value property taxes are based on) is too high and having them lowered, you can save money on the taxes paid. We went down to the tax office and requested that the taxes be reduced to reflect the value we paid for the property rather than the current assessed value of around $500,000 that was listed on the books at the tax office. This led to a major bump in our net income.

This is what the numbers looked like 3 years later:

Purchase price: $218,000
Gross income: $ 106,000
Net income: $ 50,339

Down payment: $50,000 + $5,000 (closing cost) = $55,000

Net after mortgage: $34,539
Cash-on-cash return: 62.79%

Again, as you can see, making improvements that enable you to raise rents, while cutting expenses, can increase the overall return dramatically over time.

It was with this purchase that Denio and I came up with the name of our company. After going back and forth with a few others, such as the initials of our names, we came up with Delking. Del is from DeLaurentis, Denio's last name, and King, of course, is from mine. It worked well enough. With every purchase, we put the new building in a separate LLC (Limited Liability Company), and mostly they start with Delking and the property address, such as Delking 398 Church St. LLC.

After settling into our new office, we began thinking once again about the blue six-family building on the corner. A few months had passed since our original call, when they said it was under contract, but the FOR SALE sign was still posted to the side of the building, so we gave it another shot. This time the realtor told us the building was available. Den and I were wary of the deal because we couldn't figure out why the building wasn't selling when the positive cash return seemed so obvious. Finally, we decided that we had to go through with it because we'd be kicking ourselves for not doing so every time we drove by.

This is what the numbers looked like based on the asking price:

Asking price: $165,000
Gross income: $ 34,800
Net income: $ 22,611
Cap rate: 13.7%

Down payment: $41,250 + $5,000 (closing cost) = $46,250
Net after mortgage: $11,411
Cash-on-cash return: 24.67%

The numbers fit our criteria just fine, and the location was great. It was on a main road, across from St. Mary's Catholic Church. Plus, it was just three buildings away from our first deal. Because of the proximity between the three properties, one superintendent or maintenance worker could handle all three buildings, thus saving us the time and expense of having to hire one for each property.

We offered $125,000, he countered with $133,000, and we shook on it.

This is what the numbers looked like based on the purchase price:

Asking price: $133,000
Gross income: $ 34,800
Net income: $ 22,611
Cap rate: 17%

Down payment: $33,250 + $3,000 (closing cost) = $36,250
Net after mortgage: $13,548
Cash-on-cash return: 35.41%

With this deal, there was nothing but upside. The day we closed we began a complete renovation on one of the apartments, and within three years we put in new ceramic tile, wood floors, new cabinets, and new bathrooms into most of the other units. This enabled us to increase the rent by $200 for each tenant, which added up to an additional $1200 per month.

Looking back, we still laugh about how we had asked the seller, Denis, to replace a window after the walk-through. He said he would, and when we came back, we saw that he had replaced it with a window from one of the other rooms. Then, when we asked him if we could see the tenants file, he said that he was a "little light on the paperwork" but would show us what he had. He opened the trunk of his Cadillac, took out his briefcase, and handed us an empty folder. He didn't even have one rent receipt on record. We ended up forming a friendship with Denis, as well as his son, Steve, and still meet once in a while for lunch.

Here is a look at the numbers after the rent increase:

Asking price: $133,000
Gross income: $ 49,000
Net income: $ 33,154

Down payment: $33,250 + $3,000 (closing cost) = $36,250
Net after mortgage: $24,104
Cash-on-cash return: 63%

If we take into account the money spent on repairs—approximately $8,000 over two years—it would decrease our return to 52%. So it would actually look like this:

Down payment: $33,250 + $3,000 (closing cost) = $36,250 + $8,000 = $44,250

Net after mortgage: $24,104
Cash-on-cash return: 52%

After about eight months, Den and I had spent all the money from our refinance and equity line. In total, the purchase price of the four buildings amounted to $355,000:

Building #1: Purchase price $400,000; down payment and CC: $110,000.
Building #2: Purchase price $575,000; down payment and CC: $153,750.
Building #3: Purchase price $218,000; down payment and CC: $ 55,000.
Building #4: Purchase price $133,000; down payment and CC: $ 36,250.

This money came from the refinance of our houses: $160,000 ($80,000 each); and the equity lines we took out: $186,000 ($93,000 each), for a total of $346,000, or $173,000 each. Any additional funds came out of the monthly cash flow. Let's take a look at the starting cash flow:

Building #1: Net after mortgage $30,000
Building #2: Net after mortgage $40,469
Building #3: Net after mortgage $26,190
Building #4: Net after mortgage $13,548

For a total of $110,207, or $55,103 each, or 31.85% on our investment.

Now let's take a look at the numbers on the original buildings three years later, assuming we did not refinance and pull out all of the money we had originally put in:

Building #1: Net after mortgage $44,165
Building #2: Net after mortgage $49,696
Building #3: Net after mortgage $52,751
Building #4: Net after mortgage $26,000

This would bring us to a total of $172,612, or $86,306 each, or 49.88% on our investment per year, not including appreciation or principal paydown on the mortgage.

It was at this time that I began to reflect on my new career. The success was really beginning to take shape, and I was starting to see that I was building a secure future. Making a living by owning income-producing property, where an asset was producing cash flow, as opposed to having to generate income as a salesman, broker or employee, is night and day. I now felt a greater sense of security, because I was responsible for my own vocation, unlike working for someone else or for a corporation, in which your vocation is steered from somewhere in the top rung of the corporation. Having gotten my feet wet, I was now ready to dive in headfirst.

Chapter Nine
Our Fifth Building: The Key that Opened the Golden Gate

"Now that we're out of our own money, how we do our fifth deal will be the key to opening the golden gate, whether it's a no-money-down deal, cross-collateralizing our other properties, or joining up with investors and silent partners."
– *Kevin Kingston, discussing Delking's growth strategy*

"It is common sense to take a method and try it; if it fails, admit it frankly and try another. But above all, try something."
– *Franklin D. Roosevelt*

Around the start of 2002, most of the Realtors in Dutchess County who specialized in investment property knew we were on the prowl for deals. I would call them weekly, if not more, to find out if anything new came on the market. One warm spring morning while Den and I were strategizing on my patio about the four buildings we owned, the phone rang. It was Stu, a go-getting energetic real estate broker for Re/Max. He said, "Kevin, I found you guys a deal. It just came on the market today." Without hesitation, I urged him to fax over the listing to my home fax. I also drilled him for the numbers: the number of units, gross income, expenses, and most important, the net income. Low and behold, the deal made sense.

When I got off the phone and told Den about it, I remember him being a little overwhelmed. His response was that he was all tapped out and had no money left for another deal. I told him not to worry and that we'd think of something. One thing I learned from my time on Wall

Street and from reading tons of books about real estate titans is, if the deal is good enough, finding the money is never a problem.

Let's take a look at the numbers:

Asking price: $389,000
Gross income: $ 67,740
Net income: $ 43,386
Cap rate: 11.15%

Down payment: $97,250 + $10,000 (closing cost) = $107,250

Net after mortgage: $19,206
Cash-on-cash return: 17.9%

The cap rate and cash-on-cash return did not quite fit our criteria, but the apartments were rented well below the market rate, and we knew with Super Den re-modeling each apartment, we could raise the rents by $100 to $200. Now the problem was where to find the $107,250. And adding a few bucks for repairs would realistically bring this number to $115,000.

I figured that with a starting net income of $21,309, we could do the improvements over time and increase the rents. On top of that, it was within a half mile from our four other buildings; this again would add to our economies of scale. So I showed the deal to a friend of mine and told him we would give him a preferential return of 12 percent on his money and half the equity. Without even taking a look at the property, he was in. He wrote a check for the $20,000 deposit on the spot. Stu, the broker, was elated because we were the first people to whom he had shown the property. He made his commission with one phone call. We got the price down to $355,000, or $29,500 a unit.

Here are the numbers based on the purchase price:

Asking price: $355,000
Gross income: $ 67,740
Net income: $ 43,386
Cap rate: 12.22%

Down payment: $97,250 + $10,000 (closing cost) + $7,750 (repairs) = $115,000
Net after mortgage: $21,309
Cash-on-cash return: 18.52%

When we closed on this deal, we knew we had the combination to the safe. We had our formula for growth. All we needed to do was find deals that came close to our criteria and show them to friends and family and give them a fair return on their money as well as a slice of the equity in the deal. This would let us grow, and make no mistake: We are builders, people that love the feeling from building a business. The deals, however, were getting harder to come by, and the returns were getting lower. The bottom line for us was the cash flow. We figured that appreciation would be an added benefit; as long as the deal had good cash flow, we wouldn't get hurt. This was a key concept for us, especially as we continued to grow on the fast track. As long as we had tenants paying rents, the cash flow would keep coming in. If we came across tough times and needed a cushion, meaning not be dependant on something, such as the sale of a property or completion of a development, in order to keep the business going. In reading about real estate giants of the past, most got into trouble because of overleveraging non-cash-flow properties. Take the Reichmann's and Olympia and York, for example. They built the largest real estate empire in the history of the world in the shortest amount of time imaginable. At their pinnacle they were worth over $10 billion and thus became one of the wealthiest families in the world, right behind the royal family in Britain. What defeated them in the end, even though it was comparable to the way they had initially gained their wealth, was betting it all on their latest development. Canary Wharf in London was a massive project, and they had to cross-collateralize most of their other holdings to keep the project going. The problem was, there was not enough cash flow to cover the massive debt they took on.

Other examples include Donald Trump, whose Trump Hotels & Casino Resorts went into bankruptcy protection in the 1990s and had to reorganize the rest of his debt with the banks to avoid a full scaled meltdown. Then there is real estate magnate William Zeckendorf, who revamped the look of Long Island following the Civil War. Some of his properties included the Chrysler Building, Chase Manhattan Plaza, and Denver's Mile High Center. Under his leadership, Webb & Knapp in Manhattan built $3 billion worth of commercial projects. But in 1963 the bubble burst. Both men overleveraged their properties, and when the market went sour, they didn't have enough cash flow to carry the enormous debt.

There is nothing like the leverage available in the real estate market. If the market is going your way, the returns can blow your socks off. Let's say you buy a $1,000,000 building and it increases 50 percent. That's a $500,000 gain. If you put 20 percent down, or $200,000, that 50 percent gain in the value of the building is a 250 percent gain. It is even possible to negotiate a deal with 15 percent down or less on buildings with good cash flow. In the following example, with 10 percent down, you would be up 500 percent on your $100,000.

Purchase price: $1,000,000
Down payment: $ 100,000
50% appreciation: $ 500,000
Return: $500,000 / $100,000 = 500%

There is nothing better than having a leveraged property appreciate. And there is nothing worse than having a leveraged property, with no cash flow, depreciate. At least if you have the cash flow, you have income, even if times get so bad that the property is not profitable. It is better than not having any cash flow and being dependant on selling something in a soft market. With that said, our motto is, Leverage up! But do it with income properties that have a comfortable cushion in the cash flow or, even better, a property that has some sort of upside or way of increasing the cash flow.

As I've already mentioned, we were able to improve the properties and thus able to increase the rents. This added to the cash flow. Let me explain how I structure a typical deal. Here are the key points:

- Investor puts up all the money for the down payment.
- He gets a preferential return of between (6% and 12% on the investment).
- Then there is a fill-up, meaning we get the rest of the profit until our amount equals what the investor is getting.
- The rest is split in direct proportion to ownership.
- Upon sale, the investor gets their original investment back first.
- The rest is then split in direct proportion to ownership.

Let's walk through the structure of our fifth deal:

- Investor put up $115,000.
- Investor receives the first $13,800 of profit (called a preferential return).
- Delking receives the next $13,800 of profit (called the fill up).
- Any additional profit is split according to ownership (in this case, 50 / 50, but on future deals it changed to: 75% Delking / 25% investor)
- Profits are paid monthly.
- Delking manages the property.
- Investor is passive and has no involvement in the day-to-day decisions.
- Delking prefers keeping it to one investing partner per deal.

We call this the Delking Plan. Our investors are extremely pleased with how it has been working out. We can't do deals fast enough for them. They love the concept of owning real estate and getting a monthly check, yet not dealing with the day-to-day management. The deals are getting harder and harder to find, and the preferential return has come down a bit, but creating cash flow from real estate without much involvement is still the best deal in town (in our opinion).

For us it is the ultimate leverage. We are basically buying a piece of property with our reputation. We take great pride in our growing portfolio of properties and give them extra care. We believe if we put a little extra care into them, it goes a long way, as far as our reputation. Nothing pays better dividends than a good reputation. This saying sums up our feelings about dealing with investors as well as tenants. It's important to pay attention to detail and to do what you say you will do. This is the reason the seller of the first building we bought came back to us to sell us our second building and again, three years later, when he was selling his last building. On our third purchase from him, he was so confident in us and our reputation as a stand-up company, he offered to hold a second mortgage for $300,000, allowing us to purchase the building for $775,000 with as little as 10 percent down.

Another example of going the extra mile refers to our investor. Sometimes, for a month or two, the building may not have the cash flow to continue the payments. According to the operating agreement, we would be perfectly fine to skip a payment or two, because of a vacancy or an extra expense the property is incurring because of the cost of repairs or improvements. However, we eat the loss, carry a balance on the books and collect when the property is more profitable. As Charlie Munger says in his book, *Damn Right, Behind the Scenes with Berkshire Hathaway Billionaire Charlie Munger,* "Do the best you can do. Never tell a lie. If you say you're going to do it, get it done. Nobody gives a shit about an excuse. Leave for a meeting early. Don't be late, but if you are late, don't bother giving people excuses. Just apologize. They're due an apology, but they're not interested in an excuse."

Chapter Ten
Deals Six and Seven: Ready, Fire, Aim

"Timid men are more likely to be moved to trepidation than daring in the face of great opportunities."

– *Henry Kissinger*

"Today's put-off objectives reduce tomorrow's achievements."

– *Winston Churchill*

We came upon our next two deals within 10 minutes of each other, and we had accepted offers for both within the hour, before we had any partners lined up or had even seen the properties. I'd been working the phones for months calling real estate brokers, and Den and I were checking the papers and searching on-line as well, coming up dry. It took us six months to find our first deal, and then the next four were discovered and completed rapid-fire. So hitting a dry patch for a few months was to be expected. When the call finally came from a broker, we were excited, to say the least. Walt had a 24-unit building in Hyde Park on the market. We moved fast and offered what we thought made sense. We figured that we'd worry about details later. While speaking with Walt, he mentioned that another buyer had pulled out of this deal due to another 24-unit building he was going to purchase, also in Hyde Park. Walt was hesitant to release any details of the other deal, but after persistent questioning on my part, he caved in. At that moment, sight unseen, I made an offer on that one as well. Both offers were accepted immediately.

When I called Den to tell him that the sellers had accepted offers on the two 24-unit complexes in Hyde Park, he just laughed.

After filling him in, he became excited, and we went to check them out the next day. The returns were a little less than our criteria called for, but for the sake of growth and expansion, and taking into account that they were both in good locations, we made exceptions. One of the properties was on Route 9, directly across the street from the Culinary Institute of America and up the street from Marist College. The other was on its own private dead-end street.

It all seemed a bit too easy, and upon seeing the properties, our initial excitement started to wane. We immediately saw that these properties needed some serious work. Luckily, by this time, we had a small crew that Den managed. He directed them on various projects, from emergency repairs to major improvements.

Furthermore, since this was the first time we were leaning heavily on investors for money, we learned some valuable lessons we will never forget.

The first is, ***Beware of Wall Street–collateralized conduit-type loans.*** A conduit loan backed by a Wall Street lender has an appeal, in that the rates are usually a bit lower than a conventional bank and the terms a bit more favorable. Where most banks want to see 25 percent down or close to it, a Wall Street lender may get you into a deal with as little as 15 percent down. They may be more willing to amortize the loan over 30 years, as opposed to 20 or 25 years. The longer the amortization, the less the monthly payment, and therefore the greater the cash flow. It also means the less principal you pay down over the term of the loan. For these benefits, you lock yourself into the loan for the term, say 5 or 10 years. If you want to sell or refinance, there can be a large prepayment penalty. They will allow the loan to be assumed if you are selling, after they approve the buyer, of course. These are all things you can live with, more or less. However, be forewarned: Their loyalty lies with the investors, not the borrowers. They will give the borrower just enough in the form of terms to get the deal done. Then, if you want to know how much the prepayment penalty will cost, they charge $250 (at least in our case). They will sell and trade the loan sometime annually. I believe that over three years, we have had four banks handling the mortgage. They also won't hesitate to walk from the deal at the ninth inning. So if the deal needs repairs, be careful. They may also require a large repair reserve, which you may not find out about until just before closing. This can be a problem with funding if the cash is not readily available. All and all, it's a give-and-take. So know what you're getting into.

The second lesson is, ***Budget more for repairs than you think you need.*** With one of the Hyde Park deals, we needed to replace a septic system and do extensive repairs on the well-water system. We were able to refinance and pull out enough money to handle these repairs, because the market was moving in our direction. If we did not have access to that equity through refinancing, we may have been in a bit of a bind.

Third, ***either write your own contract or make damn sure you understand every line of it.*** The contract is a crucial first step in a real estate deal. We realize this more and more with each transaction we do. If you are the buyer, the key phrases to be wary of in the contract are "as is," "time is of the essence," "on or before," "no mortgage contingency," and most importantly, the dates. Make sure you understand all the terms and deadlines, and the implications if they are not met. If you are the seller, you may want to have these words in the contract to protect you and make sure the deal moves along as scheduled.

Lastly, and perhaps the most priceless lesson of all, refers to loan commitments: ***Be sure to understand the terms and implications of the mortgage contingency in the contract***. Again, if you are a buyer, you want one and if you are a seller you would rather not put one in the contract, this way you would help insure the buyer feels confident about getting the deal done. We were very close to losing one of the Hyde Park deals, along with our deposit. After being issued a loose commitment and running up inspection, application, and appraisal fees, as well as wasting precious time, our Wall Street lender walked away from the deal. Just like that, after five months of poking along, they said no-can-do. If the contract had not been protecting us with a mortgage contingency, we would have lost our deposit. Even though the lender had a loan commitment, they still backed out, and the way the commitment was worded, they could have backed out if they didn't like the way we sneezed

After the Wall Street lender walked, we went with a credit union, which used the reports already prepared by the previous lender. The annual interest rate was 9 percent as opposed to 6 percent, but the deal closed in three weeks. Although the transaction did not end up being as smooth as we had anticipated, we did learn some very valuable lessons along the way, and most of all, the Hyde Park properties have appreciated well in the short time we owned them.

Chapter Eleven
Florida: The Sun Belt and the Baby Boomers

"Another lot was sold successively for $2,500, $7,800, $10,000, $17,500 and finally, $35,000—the last purchaser being the man who sold it for $2,500. A property owner on the street was asked what his property was worth and said, 'Well, it was worth about $30,000 at nine o'clock this morning. But at ten o'clock the lot next to mine sold for $40,000, so I suppose it ought to bring about $50,000, as it is now ten minutes past twelve.' "

—*From* More Extraordinary Popular Delusions and the Madness of Crowds *by Joseph Bulgatz, referring to the Florida land boom in the mid 1920s*

Starting around 2006, a baby boomer will retire every few seconds for roughly the next eighteen years. This means more people will be heading south by the busload. The most sought-after places will be those with the warmest climates and those closest to water. It doesn't take a brain surgeon to figure out that this will increase the demand for Florida real estate. Both the east and west coasts of the Sunshine State will see a hell of a run over the next several years. Things will inevitably turn into a frenzy, and you will know it's reached that point when you see people doing real estate deals on napkins at bars and cafés. Until then, it's buckle-up-and-hold-on-for-the-ride.

Den and I usually hit the gym in the morning for a quick workout before heading upstairs to the office. It's during these workouts that we fantasized about owning a property in Florida. We would say, "Just think of it. We could head down for a day or two, check on the property, hit the beach for a swim, maybe squeeze a round of golf in during the winter, and it's a business trip."

Shortly thereafter, we started investigating a few deals on Florida's east coast. We concentrated our attention between Palm Beach and South Beach, east of the intercoastal, a.k.a. the Gold Coast. It's not like there were deals all over; you had to search for them. And if you looked hard enough, you could find a 10 percent cap rate, which we finally did, in Hollywood Beach.

The beach area lagged behind some of the more modern communities, as far as developments went, and it was as if it had been asleep for the last few decades, especially when compared to Miami real estate, just 15 minutes south, or going north, up the coast to Boca Raton and Palm Beach. South Beach and Ft. Lauderdale were pricey as well, making no sense as far as cash flow. But in Hollywood Beach there was, and still is, a 1940s look to the boardwalk, and most of the deals needed a lot of work, which was fine with us, because Super Den was ready to spring into action. But the deals there basically fit our criteria.

After researching every deal in the area, we zeroed in on the Barbizon Motel on A1A, just south of Hollywood Boulevard. We purchased this for $820,000 in November of 2002. We had an investor come in as a partner and closed the deal with the seller holding a $500,000 mortgage with a 30 year amortization and a 6 1/2 % rate. It is a 17-unit motel with the best view of the intercoastal on Ocean Drive, or A1A. You can sit in the office and look out at the water, right where it opens up to a lake called South Lake. Boats and jet-skiers by the dozens go by all day long. Every other spot on Ocean Drive has a view obstructed by buildings on the other side of A1A. The world-famous Hollywood Beach Boardwalk is also just steps away. The boardwalk is two and a half miles long, and the south side begins right at the Barbizon. This section of the beach is absolutely beautiful. It's quiet and serene yet only a five-minute walk to all the shops, cafés, and restaurants on the boardwalk.

Whenever I go down, I make it a point to run in the morning right after my coffee. Then I sit on the beach for a few minutes and clear my head. This is my favorite time. While I sit there and contemplate how different things are now from my days on Wall Street, it becomes mind-boggling. Just a few years ago I would have been a fanatic about making sure my cell phone was working and busy checking in with the office every chance I got. Or I would worry about the market or the latest stock I just bought. Every time I went on vacation, I'd mentally prepare myself for a blow-up of some sort waiting for me upon my return.

It's been almost three years now, and so far the Barbizon has worked out well. We are paying the investor 10 percent as well as an additional profit for Delking Hospitalities LLC (the name of the LLC through which we purchased the building). Besides a decent cash flow, the purchase gave us reasons to head to Florida. We were able to find good managers, which helped us tremendously. A buddy of mine from Gruntal, Angelo Pomes, came down to help manage the place and get us up and running while enjoying Florida for about six months. Angelo is a laid-back Italian who immensely enjoys his cigarettes and espresso. The word "rush" does not exist, as far as he is concerned. When we were heading down for the closing, he was supposed to meet us at the airport. He showed up two days later. Together we implemented some great systems, like the daily sheet, which showed the check-ins and -outs and the money taken in for the day. This sheet is faxed to our office daily at the beginning and end of each day. He also created a weekly bank deposit form that gives us a breakdown of the amount deposited and the expenses for the week.

The funny thing is, if you ask five people what they think about Florida real estate, most of them will say they are looking for something like a condo or a townhouse down there, or they already have one in the family. My mother-in-law bought a lot in Palm Coast from a door-to-door salesman in White Plains. He worked for ITT Corporation, which developed the area in the 1980s. She paid a $15,000 purchase price, financed, of course, so the payments were affordable at $170 or so a month. With interest, the total payments were just under $25,000. The quotes and offers she has been getting from Realtors over the years were as low as $4,000 in the late 1990s and was recently just over $95,000.

Florida real estate has a certain appeal to it as opposed to most places in America. People love to fantasize about retiring to warm weather and enjoying a stable climate all year-round. Not just people from the United States but Canadians and Europeans as well. Their winter is even rougher than ours. And because Europe basically shuts down during the month of August, you also have an influx of Europeans enjoying the south Florida sunshine.

So Florida attracts the retirees, the people who just want to own a place to go a few times a year, and the younger population, who move there because they want a lifestyle change. The population in south Florida is growing rapidly, and this growth will only accelerate as the baby boomers start to hit their peak propensity to retire. I drove from Hollywood Beach to South Beach taking A1A South and counted 22 new buildings going up on the beach. All the cranes looked like something from outer-space shooting up 30 to 40 stories in every which direction. For the most part, these are condos with 30, 40, or more floors and are mostly pre-sold before the builder even breaks ground. The demand is there and will continue for the next several years. Sooner or later, however, it will most likely end the way most demographics- and speculative-driven booms end—in some sort of bust.

To protect Delking, we are not leveraging up on deals that don't make any sense cash flow–wise. We will wait until we find deals that fit our criteria, and when the return on our equity in the deals drops down to the single digits, we will look to unload. Our view is, if you have capital at risk earning less than 10 percent or so, take a close look at it even if the equity is from appreciation.

I recently went down to play golf with two of my cousins, Enzo and Ennio, along with Ennio's buddy, Vinny. We left at eight in the morning and were on the course by noon. Afterward we dined in style with a few bottles of wine while recapping the day's events. Then we repeated the drill for the next two days. In the mornings, it was off to Georgio's, the French Bakery on Ocean Avenue, located in the middle of Hollywood Beach. They have the best fresh bread and croissants I have ever had. They have a whole assortment of cheeses, from floor to ceiling. I would highly recommend it if you ever visit Hollywood Beach!

You can't beat the getaways that owning property in Hollywood encourages. It truly is a rejuvenating day or two, even though it is a business-oriented trip. We do spend a lot of time looking at other deals and scouting out areas. One of my favorite times, believe it or not, is on the plane, because it's the only time I'm able to sit down and read for a few hours. My two sons, Codi and Luca, who are three and two, respectively, demand Daddy's attention whenever I am at home, not to mention my wife, who points out that she also exists somewhere between upstate New York and south Florida.

Chapter Twelve
Deal 9: Expanding in Poughkeepsie

"As I grow older, I pay less attention to what men say; I just watch what they do."

– Andrew Carnegie

"Skill to do comes of doing."

– Ralph Waldo Emerson

Our ninth deal came about from our old friend Stu (the Realtor from deal five), along with another Realtor in the area, Nader. They were offering a 33-unit brick building a few houses away from our second deal, the 18-unit brick building. The purchase price was $1,450,000, or just under $44,000 a unit, and we needed about $450,000 as a down payment. Although the current owner was not much of a landlord and had neglected the property, the numbers made sense and fit our criteria, so we decided to make a go of it. In true Delking fashion, we made an offer over the phone based on the numbers. The fact that it was our largest deal so far was a minor thought for us because we had the formula down cold. As long as we could continue finding deals where the numbers made sense we planned to continue purchasing, and we weren't looking for smaller deals.

We received the funds from an investor, and everything began moving according to plan. However, as we neared the closing, the seller started playing games and getting greedy. We figured he must have received a higher offer, because he began to demand more money in order to follow through with the sale.

Even though the contract is a legally binding document, our situation was such that we could not afford to tie up our funds while we argued out the legality of his actions in court. We had accepted funds from an investor who had not received payments for an already extended period of time. For that reason, we basically caved to the seller's strong-arm tactics and settled on an extra $100,000 in the form of a second mortgage.

Delking bases its excellence on keeping its word. To us, a deal is a deal, so doing business with someone who does not keep to their end of the bargain is unsettling—but not unusual. Word is, he is currently selling another building in Poughkeepsie and is using the same tactics.

After finally closing, we realized we had our work cut out for us. We learned that if someone plays games in one area, you can expect game playing in other areas. Take, for instance, the boiler. In the oil business himself, the seller told us that the boiler had been rebuilt a few years before. After two years, it blew up. On the coldest day of the year, the thing decided to call it quits. Within an hour we were at the store renting space heaters for the tenants and had a new boiler installed the next day.

But even beyond that was the way in which he ran—or didn't run—his building. It was pure chaos. The tenants needed to be trained to pay on time and to be respectful to their neighbors. In addition, we noticed that the tenants would throw their garbage—sometimes in bags, sometimes not—right out their window and leave it on the property. When Den and I walked inside the building one day, there were four or five kids hanging on the ceiling heating pipes as though it were a jungle gym. Loud music, cursing and fighting, walking on the railings like a balance beam, writing on the hallway walls, and breaking windows—you name it, it was a real handful.

It took time and energy, but now the building runs like a Delking property should. Tenants pay on time or else let us know if there is a problem. We do repairs within a day or two and are always doing improvements to enhance the building.

So although the intention of buying new properties is to strengthen Delking's portfolio, it also provides an inner strength for Den and I. We learn from each buying experience that it's not only about numbers but also about how to stay with a commitment and follow through with a plan. Thus, we learn from each obstacle that is thrown our way and have become more insightful with each deal we close.

Chapter Thirteen
Gearing Up for Explosive Growth

"A bad plan is more likely to work than no plan at all."

"Chart your course with strategic planning. Think of your business plan as a map, with a time line and checkpoints to follow in route."

—*Jim Clayton, author of* First a Dream

In 1966 Jim Clayton followed his dream and founded Clayton Homes, which builds, sells, and leases manufactured homes and relocatable commercial and educational buildings. In his book, *First a Dream,* he wrote about how he built up his empire based on two key attributes—hard work and perseverance—and in 2003 sold his business to Berkshire Hathaway for $1.7 billion. This is a true rags-to-riches story, and it inspired me so much, I ordered extra copies and sent them to several of my business associates.

Throughout his book, Clayton stresses the importance of being organized and having a plan. Delking's mission is, "Strive to innovate and build a well-run, well-respected, profitable company that will maximize value for its partners and employees," and I think we've so far exceeded our goal. From 2000 to 2004 we grew at an annual rate of 100 percent. Below is a year-by-year breakdown of our revenue growth:

Year-by-Year Breakdown		Revenues
2000	0 units – looking for deals	$ 0.00
2001	29 units	$ 280,000
2002	98 units	$ 860,000
2003	185 units	$1,230,000
2004	352 units	$2,600,000

Now it was time to take a serious look at our infrastructure. How and where we were spending money needed to be closely evaluated; operations needed to be fine-tuned; systems and procedures needed to be implemented. We were growing all right, but our expenses were growing just as fast—even faster, in fact. Keeping expenses under control is one of the hardest things about growing a business, especially if the business is growing at such a rapid pace.

We started with our legal expense. We were annualizing to spend close to $65,000 on closings, refinances, and evictions. This did not include lease and document reviews, which included the operating agreements for each LLC (Limited Liability Company). This I was doing myself. I would form a new LLC for each property we purchased. While going over our different options, Den and I interviewed Theoni Salotto. She had years of legal experience in the real estate industry, and because she had three small children, she was looking for a job with flexibility. This worked for us, so we offered her the position of General Counsel and she accepted. She is doing great juggling family and career, and enjoys the flexibility that working for Delking offers.

Next we tackled the computer system. At the time, we had a four-computer wireless network that would go down a couple of times a month, crippling the office and bringing us all to a standstill for days. We decided to confront this problem once and for all by calling some old high school buddies, Greg Candido and Rick Monzon, who are both employed at Manhattan Information Systems. Greg's father had started this company out of his garage and grew it to an impressive business. They had a multi-computer network up and running within weeks. We could now access the network remotely with roaming profiles, and we host our own website. This sent our productivity through the roof and made our work lives much easier.

Upgrading our two-line crackpot phone system to a ten-line system with a receptionist switchboard and voicemail quickly became our next challenge. We hired a full-time office assistant to handle all of the calls and administrative duties. Our first, part-time office assistant was a high school student named Michelle, who left us to go to St. John's College in Brooklyn. Michelle's mother, Pattie, was a local Realtor who also worked as our in-house rental agent, with 352 units, we were fully engrossed with maintaining our current properties while keeping an eye out for any new deals, and we had no time to worry about finding tenants or working with outside Realtors to fill any vacancies. She agreed to work for us part-time while showing her own listings, which gave her the flexibility to be able to care for her five children. Fortunately, during the holidays, Michelle still comes back to help out. We were now getting used to delegating the major duties we had been dealing with for the past four years and even went so far as hiring a bookkeeper, named Zoila, to handle all our accounting work and help out in the area of property management.

Finally, the office was operating with a solid infrastructure and we were now able to handle double, triple, and even quadruple growth of the business without a flinch. The staff was in place, so now it was time to implement some property-management software. We chose Rent Manager to help keep track of things. We were initially using QuickBooks, at the insistence of our CPA, Mat Cronin, in 2004. It was just too hard to keep track of the growing number of buildings, because you had to keep switching from building to building to view information. With Rent Manager everything is accessible at once. We needed to simplify, and specialty software was the way to go. Rent Manager allows users to log on from any location via the Internet. All the information is backed up on the server as soon as it is entered. This gives our remote property managers access to tenant information and enables them to note accounts and make changes in real time that can be viewed throughout the system. It is an invaluable tool that I would highly recommend.

Growing pains are tough to deal with. We really have a lot going on and need to delegate responsibility to dependable people. Jack Welch, in his book *Straight From the Gut,* is continuously stressing the importance of key, dependable people. That's the backbone of GE. With Jack, it's all about the people. They would have intense performance reviews, routinely firing the bottom 10 percent of performers. He says this is the hardest part of the job, but the most beneficial, because it keeps the employees focused. And he's not kidding; it is hard.

We believe that while it is important to let go of the poor performers, it is just as imperative to reward the hardworking, dedicated employees. One of our benefits is to offer employees, who have more than a year of service with Delking, a small ownership percentage of a newly purchased property. This ownership grant is not paid for at all by the employee, and the percent ownership ranges from a few percent to 5 percent of a deal. We believe this will help to retain dedicated employees while rewarding them for a job well done.

Chapter Fourteen
Understanding Amplification of Returns

"Give me a lever long enough and a fulcrum on which to place it, and I shall move the world."

– Archimedes, Pappus of Alexandria

If a property appreciates 3 percent, and an investor buys it and puts forth a down payment of 25 percent of the purchase price, his return on his investment is 12 percent. . . .

If a property appreciates 3 percent and an investor buys it and puts forth a down payment of 20 percent of the purchase price, his return on his investment is 15 percent. . . .

If a property appreciates 3 percent and an investor buys it and puts forth a down payment of 15 percent, his return on his investment is 20 percent. . . .

If a property appreciates 3 percent and an investor buys it and puts forth a down payment of 10 percent of the purchase price, his return on his investment is 30 percent. . . .

If a property appreciates 3 percent and an investor buys it and puts forth a down payment of 5 percent of the purchase price, his return on his investment is 60 percent. . . .

Get the idea?

However, this amplification can work *against* investors as well. A small drop in prices could basically eliminate all the equity in a leveraged property. Let's say you put 10 percent into a deal and borrow the other 90 percent, and the value of the property drops by 10 percent. You will have lost all your equity.

Fortunately, there are a few ways to protect yourself. If your loan is amortized, you pay down some of the principal every month (as opposed to just paying the interest with an interest-only loan, which many are using these days to enhance cash flow). Doing so will build a larger equity base. Hopefully, the mortgage payment can come from cash flow- from rents you're taking in. You won't notice your overall loan decreasing by much in the beginning, but it will decrease more rapidly over time. Another way to protect yourself is through forced appreciation, which we discussed earlier, in Chapter 7. But perhaps the best way to protect yourself is to make sure you have enough cash flow on the deal to ride out a real estate slump. This way, the depreciation in real estate prices will not hurt you as far as being able to pay your bills on the property while still having some cash flow left for yourself.

Do the best you can to look into the future and ask yourself, "If this tenant leaves, will we still be able to pay our bills?" Make a judgment call. Work through the numbers with lower monthly rents to make sure the deal would still make sense if you had to lower rents to attract tenants. The main thing is to look for deals that have a nice cushion in the cash flow. A cushion or a buffer, meaning, room for error, since things rarely go as planned and there are always unexpected expenses.

Now let's get back to some hypothetical examples.

If a piece of property appreciates 3 percent and an investor buys it and puts forth a down payment of 20 percent of the purchase price, his return on his investment is 15 percent.

If an investor, through forced appreciation and market appreciation, owns a property that over a few years appreciates by 30 percent and he put down 20 percent originally, he has a return of 150 percent on his money invested:

Original purchase price: $1,000,000
Down payment: $ 200,000
Appreciation: $ 300,000
Return: 150%

This is not taking into account the principal paydown over the few years and the cash flow, assuming there was any.

Furthermore, let's say this investor refinances this property and pulls out his original investment of $200,000. The new mortgage payment will most likely go up, because he is borrowing more money, but let's say the rents also went up, so therefore the effect can be absorbed without a problem. (We have actually refinanced a building and pulled out $300,000 and had the mortgage payment go down. This was because of a drop in interest rate and an extended amortization period.)

Now let's say this investor, the super-aggressive young man that he is, buys another property and goes through the whole rigmarole again. And just for the fun of it, let's say he does it again after that—all the while continuing to improve all properties by forcing appreciation and enjoying the cash flow.

This is how things should look:

Original investment = $200,000

Deal 1: Return of 150% (after a few years, not including cash flow and principal paydown).

Deal 2: Same as Deal 1. Put $200,000 into it, improved property, refinanced, and pulled the $200,000 back out for another deal. Let's assume this deal had the same 30% appreciation for a total return of 150% to the investor.

Deal 3: Same as Deal 1 and 2. $200k in, $200k out, 30% appreciation = 150% to investor.

Assuming no further appreciation on Deal 1 and 2 after the 30% move that allowed him to put the equity out, the total return would look like this:

Initial equity investment: $200,000
Appreciation in Deal 1: $300,000
Appreciation in Deal 2: $300,000
Appreciation in Deal 3: $300,000

Total Appreciation: $900,000, or 450% on the original $200,000

As you can see, a 30 percent move in the property is amplified to the extent the investor was able to borrow money in the form of a mortgage, and then remortgage or refinance to pull his gains out and parlay them into another deal, and so on.

If we assume these deals had a cash flow of 20 percent on the money down, or a cash-on-cash return of 20 percent, we could add that on to the total return, per property, per year.

Now you may be thinking that these deals are hard to come by or that this can be only one best-case scenario in a million, but I can assure you that this is very possible in the real world.

For instance, here is a real-life example:

Scott Jerutis, my buddy who explained his first deal to me over and over again and who inspired me to forge ahead with a future in real estate, started out with a $115,000 down payment (see Chapter 7). He purchased an 11-unit apartment complex. Within a few years, he was able to refinance and pull out more than $250,000 in equity, which he used to buy a commercial property in White Plains on Post Road. Within another two years he was able to add value to his commercial deal by utilizing empty space on the side of the building and installing a 3500-square-foot storefront. He then refinanced this property, using the forced appreciation, and pulled out over $600,000, of which he used a portion to purchase a $2.3 million office complex, along with some other investors, in Ossining, New York, for $2,300,000.

As you can see, he's amplifying his returns through leveraging and then re-leveraging.

Within five years he sold the original 11-unit apartment complex, making close to a million-dollar profit, which he then put into a shopping center in Chicago for $5,000,000. This sends his cash flow through the roof. He leveraged up, in an up real estate market, with a keen eye on situations to which he could add value. With the office building, he filled the empty space, which brings the value up to over $4,000,000. He is now looking to develop shopping centers in the Chicago area and possibly in Dutchess County, New York.

Now let's turn again to the hypothetical example.

So far, for the most part, I spoke about leveraging up using one's own money for the down payment. Let's examine what would happen if the super-aggressive young man in the above example, who did the three deals with his $200,000, had set his sights a bit higher. Let's say he found a $10,000,000 deal that needed $2,000,000 as a down payment.

After putting the numbers on paper and examining them ten ways from Sunday, he figures the deal should have a16 percent cash-on-cash return. To be safe, he knocks 3 percent of the return off and sets it aside for reserves. This brings the initial cash-on-cash return to 13 percent.

He offers an 8 percent preferential return to a few investors. That is, they get the first $160,000 of profit, which would be 8 percent of their investment ($2,000,000 x 8% = $160,000). Then he would get the next $160,000 of profit, and any additional profit would be split in proportion to ownership.

He splits the ownership or equity up by giving the investors 25 percent and himself 75 percent. This is also how any appreciation would be split. The investors love the fact that they are getting 8 percent and owning a piece of a nice property that will hopefully appreciate over time.

Upon a sale, the investors would get the $2,000,000 back first, and then any profit would be split according to ownership.

In this situation, any appreciation would have an infinite return to the organizer. If the building appreciated 30 percent, or $3,000,000, he would have equity of $2,250,000.

$3,000,000 x 75% ownership = $2,250,000

If we add one of these deals to the other three, then:

Initial equity investment: $200,000

Appreciation in Deal 1: $ 300,000
Appreciation in Deal 2: $ 300,000
Appreciation in Deal 3: $ 300,000
Appreciation in Deal 4: $2,250,000

Total Appreciation: $3,150,000 or 1,575% on the original $200,000

This is how the really, really big money is made in real estate—using leverage and other people's money. Don't be misled; there are a lot of details, organization, and frustration that goes into putting deals together and running them. You need to be a special type of person to handle the pressure of multimillion-dollar deals. The way I look at it is, pressure is a part of life; you're going to have to deal with pressure in whatever you do anyway, so why not swing for the fences? If you don't swing the bat, you'll never hit that ball. Things may not happen as planned in life, but great things are guaranteed not to happen if you don't ever take that first step.

Chapter Fifteen
Principal Paydown: A Forced Savings Plan

"Everything I've done I've copied from someone else."
—Sam Walton, founder of Wal-Mart

"Fortune assists the brave."
—Terence

In George Clason's best-selling book, *The Richest Man in Babylon,* he argues that the sure way to wealth is to save a small percentage of your monthly earnings every month before paying even the first bill. This theme is repeated again and again in many books centered on creating wealth for oneself, such as *The Millionaire Next Door* by Thomas Stanley. The concept calls for people to pay themselves first by putting away at least 10 percent of their earnings in some sort of savings plan to be invested and grow over time.

This is indeed a very powerful concept that will sooner or later create real results. Let's use this concept in a hypothetical light. When you buy an investment property, or any real estate for that matter, for, say, $1,000,000, and then mortgage 80 percent or $800,000 with an interest rate of 6 percent amortized over 20 years, the monthly mortgage payment is roughly $5,731. In the early stages of the loan, the portion of this payment that goes to pay down principal on a monthly basis is roughly $732; after three years it will increase to around $900; after seven years it will rise to about $1,140. This amount, which is paying down the principal on the loan, is simultaneously building up equity in the property. I like to call this equity forced savings. It's even better when the property is an investment property where the tenants pay for all the operating expenses via their monthly rent payments.

Let's take a closer look at this example:

Purchase price	$1,000,000	
Down payment	$ 200,000	
Monthly payment	$ 5,731	(principal and interest)
Principal paydown per month	$ 732	(year 1) or $8,784 per year
Principal paydown per month	$ 900	(year 3) or $10,800 per year
Principal paydown per month	$ 1,140	(year 7) or $13,680 per year

This savings adds up over time. If you are like us, and this concept really hits home, you may do very well continuing to purchase investment properties and really put this concept to work. Even when we ran out of money, we figured out a way to continue to make new deals by bringing in partners with the Delking plan (see Chapter 9).

When you look at the numbers on multiple properties or larger deals, the monthly forced savings starts to really add up.

Chapter Sixteen
Investing in a Business vs. Running a Business vs. Owning a Business

"I think of stocks as businesses."
—Laurence Tisch, New York billionaire and philanthropist

When Larry Tisch, Berkshire Hathaway founder Warren Buffett, or Wesco's CEO Charlie Munger looks to buy a stock, they look at it as buying a piece of the company. They take a close look at the cash flow of the business and the relationship between the stock price or the market capitalization of the company and the profit in the underlying company. If these relationships are out of whack, they pass. It's that simple. They don't overpay. The idea is so basic: Pay attention to the return on monies invested. When looking at a business or a stock, the underlying question is what the return will be from operations. Appreciation will take care of itself if the company can:

1) Be bought at the right price.
2) Continue to earn a profit.

When Larry Tisch and his brother, Bob, were looking to grow in the early years, they looked at everything they could find that showed at least a 12 percent return, from hotels to summer camps to movie theaters and then finally to CBS. According to Christopher Winans, author of *The King of Cash*, Tisch's net worth is more than $1 billion. His corporate assets total more than $40 billion, and he generates almost $14 billion in annual revenue. "His thrift in the name of cash flow is legendary," Winans contends.

Too often—and believe me, I learned this the hard way—investors get caught up with the potential for appreciation and ignore the basics, like return on equity or cash flow. Many times it is a vision thing—how this technology will change the world—and they worry about the cash flow later. The argument is always that the revenues will justify the price rise, sometime in the future.

In Ben Graham's *The Intelligent Investor,* he suggests taking the last five or ten years of earnings to arrive at the value of a company. The idea of even valuing the company on next year's earnings, as is common these days, was absurd to him.

It took me a while to realize the importance of truly understanding the delicate relationship between money invested and cash flow. This was the beginning of a whole new aspect of my investment career. It was the foundation that I would build on and add leverage to, ever so delicately. Looking back, this new approach makes much more sense, as opposed to using leverage to speculate on fluctuating stocks without any concern for the down-and-dirty fundamentals of the underlying business. Sure, we all believed the products of the companies we were buying were phenomenal and had wide-reaching applications, but there has to be a limit to the premium put on even the most earth-shattering of new inventions. With this new realization, we took our real estate and investments in businesses to a whole new level.

As Robert Kiyosaki points out repeatedly in his book *Cashflow Quadrant,* there is a world of difference between owning a business and being a business owner who operates that business. When fully comprehended, this is a life-changing concept. Once you can analyze a small investment property—that is, look at the rents or income and subtract the expenses and take a good stab at what the profits should be, it's not much of a jump to be able to understand a small business, like a motel or small hotel.

It's not easy, though. Denio and I struggled with the concept for years. We still don't have it perfected, but we are working very hard to improve on the most important ingredient in being able to grow: finding key people and delegating responsibility to them. Once you have the whole cash flow and leverage concept under your belt, you will be able to grow. One of the reasons we have been including key employees in deals is that we believe it will keep them focused and loyal when, over time, their ownership portion appreciates. In turn, their example of employee participation in deals will help attract talented employees.

Trammell Crow, founder of the Trammell Crow Company, a diversified commercial real estate services firm that operates worldwide, has been very successful in offering its employees equity in the company's properties. He had hundreds and hundreds of partnerships all over the country with dependable people running them. The operator or manager would start out with 20 percent of the deal, and as the property became more profitable or they expanded in the area, his percentage would increase. In *Trammell Crow, Master Builder: The Story of America's Largest Real Estate Empire,* by Robert Sobel, Crow says that he loved putting deals together, as did Harry Helmsley. Harry once told one of his partners, who suggested that, the real estate magnate slow down on the deals, "These deals are like my grandchildren." I must agree. There is a great feeling in putting deals together, from finding them to analyzing them, then working out the particulars, like financing and the ownership structure. It is tremendously rewarding, and I truly enjoy it. Between November of 2003 and August of 2004, Delking purchased eight properties, all over the East Coast, from south Florida up to western Massachusetts. Upon closing each deal, Den and I would enjoy a three-hour lunch, then a celebratory dinner with our wives.

When looking at properties, I examine the numbers and Den goes over the structure and general condition of the building. If the numbers work and he gives me the thumbs-up on the building, we are off to the races. At times we would juggle five contracts to purchase simultaneously. After the closings, he'd say, "Congratulations and good job, buddy." And I'd reply, "Good luck!"

Sometimes, though, I am overwhelmed with all of the deals that get thrown my way each day. They come in all day long, by phone, through e-mail, and via the fax machine. As well, I always have at least one Realtor phoning about something that just came on the market. I just can't crunch the numbers fast enough, but for the most part, the returns are below our criteria, so it makes the elimination process easy.

We look at real estate deals as mini businesses. We figured out that to grow Delking, we must look for properties and businesses that do not require us to run them. In other words, we want to buy a *business*, not a job. We are taking the lead from Warren Buffett. When he buys a business, he does not want to run it or even have his people run it. He is looking for businesses that have management in place. He also makes it blatantly clear that he is looking for a simple business that he can understand. Nothing complicated, like technology companies. The bottom line, as always, is good old cash flow.

Chapter Seventeen
An All-out Buying Spree

"John Jacob Astor had participated in hundreds, even thousands, of transactions, buying, selling, leasing, renting, and lending money on real estate security."

"If Astor had a philosophy, it was to let the chips fall where they may, to make the best of opportunities and not to cry over spilt milk."

—*From* John Jacob Astor: America's First Multimillionaire
by Alex Madsen

When John Jacob Astor died, in 1848, he was declared the richest man in America. He was 84 years old, and his fortune represented more than six and a half percent of the personal wealth in the nation. A large chunk of his money was made in Manhattan real estate. He once claimed that knowing what he knows now, he would have bought the whole island of Manhattan, and when asked why he was selling a downtown piece of property that would more than likely double over the next five years, he responded by explaining that he was taking that money and buying ten times more property, which would increase tenfold in the same time frame 30 blocks north. The idea is that as the population of a major metropolis grows, it pushes the price of real estate up in an ever expanding radius.

One of my favorite sayings is, "Two ways to make a fortune are by buying whiskey by the bottle and selling it by the shot, and buying land by the acre and selling it by the lot."

As I figure it, the expanding radius of price appreciation from the major metropolis (NY City) hit Poughkeepsie right about the time we started purchasing our buildings there. A few years later, after taking into account the effect of lower interest rates, the improvements made to our properties, and the fact that most of America was afraid of the stock market and plowing money into real estate, we were sitting on a bunch of equity from some phenomenal appreciation. Best of all, because interest rates were down, we could refinance and pull out the money we had originally put into the deals and more, without sending our mortgage payment through the roof and in some cases actually reducing it.

By using our equity from our existing deals, taking on partners, and securing a bridge loan, we purchased six properties in Massachusetts, which consisted of 14 buildings, or 132 units; a 30-unit motel/inn on the beach in Hollywood Beach, Florida; and another 14-unit building in Poughkeepsie. This was an exciting time for Delking. We were in Massachusetts one day and Poughkeepsie the next, followed shortly thereafter by a flight to Florida. When I mentioned to Den that I found a deal in Utica, New York, he looked at me as if he were going to choke me.

In Economics 101, you learn that when the Federal Reserve cuts interest rates, it stimulates the economy. Conversely, when they raise interest rates, it slows the economy. While on Wall Street, I've witnessed the dramatic effects that changes in interest rates have on markets. So as the Fed started cutting rates at the end of 2000, it may have taken a while to sink in, but I eventually realized the effect an 85 percent reduction in interest rates to an almost unprecedented low would have on the economy—in particular, the real estate market.

As you can see from the chart below, from the end of 2000 to the final rate reduction in mid-2003, the Federal Funds Rate was reduced from 6.5 percent to 1 percent, or just about an 85 percent reduction over two and a half years. This was more than just a stimulus; this was a jumbo stimulus combined with a power shot that in conjunction with President Bush's tax cuts had to have one hell of an effect on things. Add the fact that so many people were discouraged with the stock market and were looking for a place to invest, our timing was perfect. The only thing I could think of to do was buy real estate. This realization coincided with our buying spree.

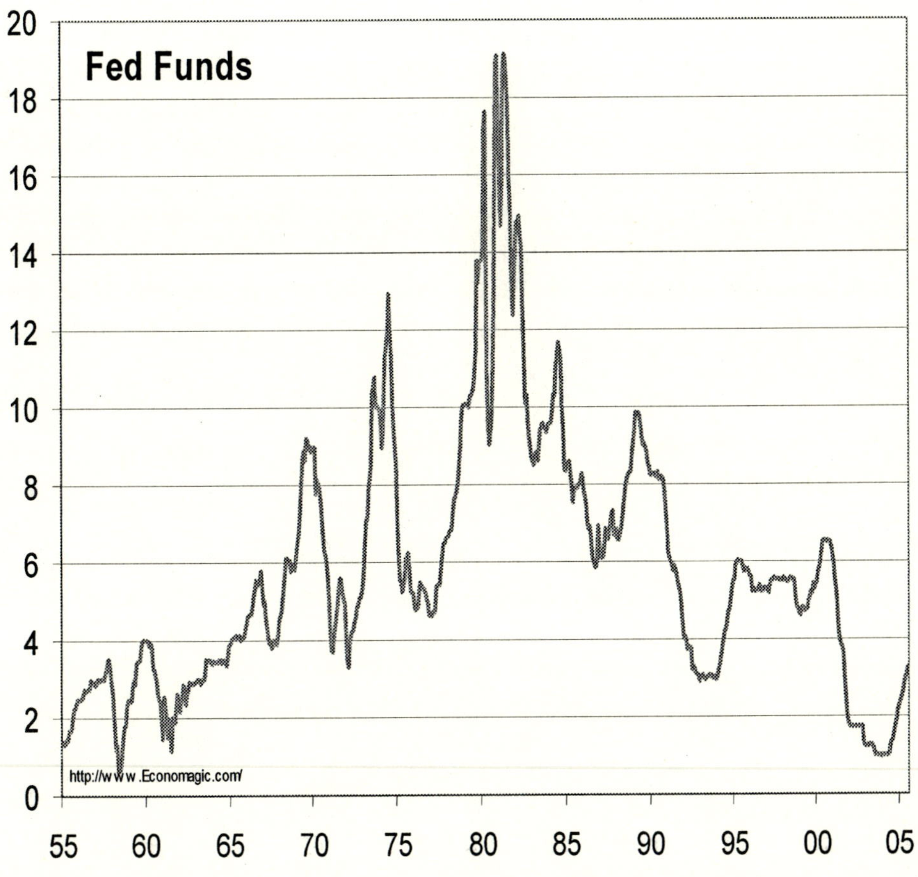

The Federal Funds Rate is the interest rate charged by banks on loans of their excess reserve funds to other banks. The Federal Reserve's ability to add or withdraw reserves from the banking system gives it close control over this rate. The percentage of the drop and the fact that it brought rates to the lowest point in our history and kept them there for a historically unprecedented period of time added to the underlying economic forces that would give the real estate market the biggest push we will probably ever see. I do not believe this push has played itself out just yet. There may very well be several years left.

Rates were kept at 1 percent for a year (from July of 2003 to July of 2004) and under 2 percent for just about three years (from December of 2001 to November of 2004). The opportunity is now. This is unprecedented. This is the time to buy real estate, particularly properties that are cash flowing. I am not talking about the Florida preconstruction condo market bonanza. That may prove to be a particularly risky sector of the overall real estate market. Real cash flow deals that have potential for improvements are much safer places to put money.

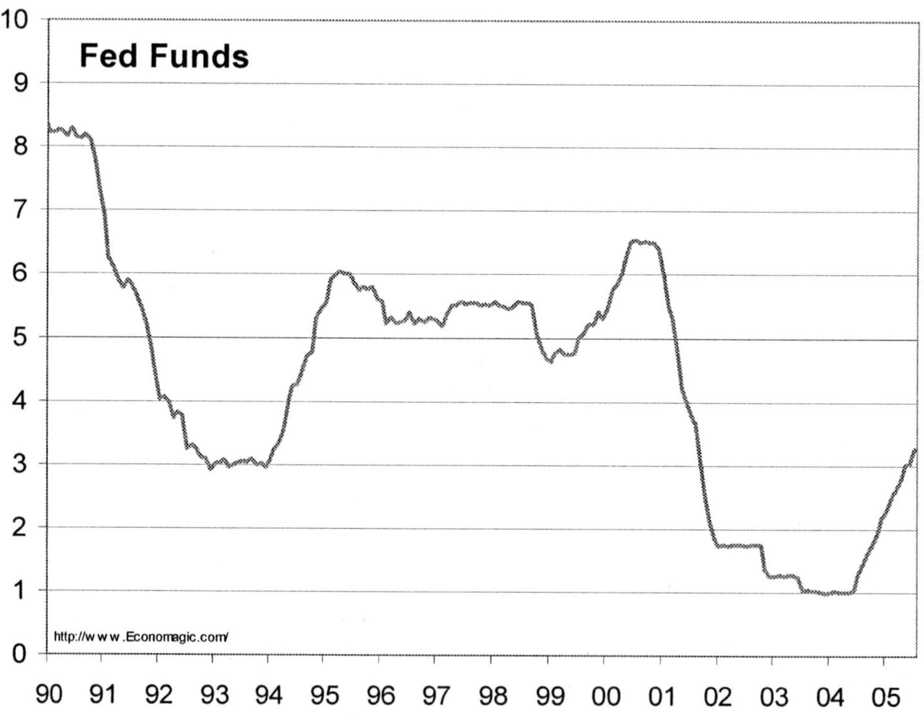

Below is the Federal Discount Rate, which is the interest rate at which an eligible financial institution may borrow funds directly from a Federal Reserve Bank. Banks whose reserves dip below the reserve requirement set by the Federal Reserve's board of governors use that money to correct their shortage. The board of directors of each reserve bank sets the discount rate every 14 days. It's considered the last resort for banks, which usually borrow from each other.

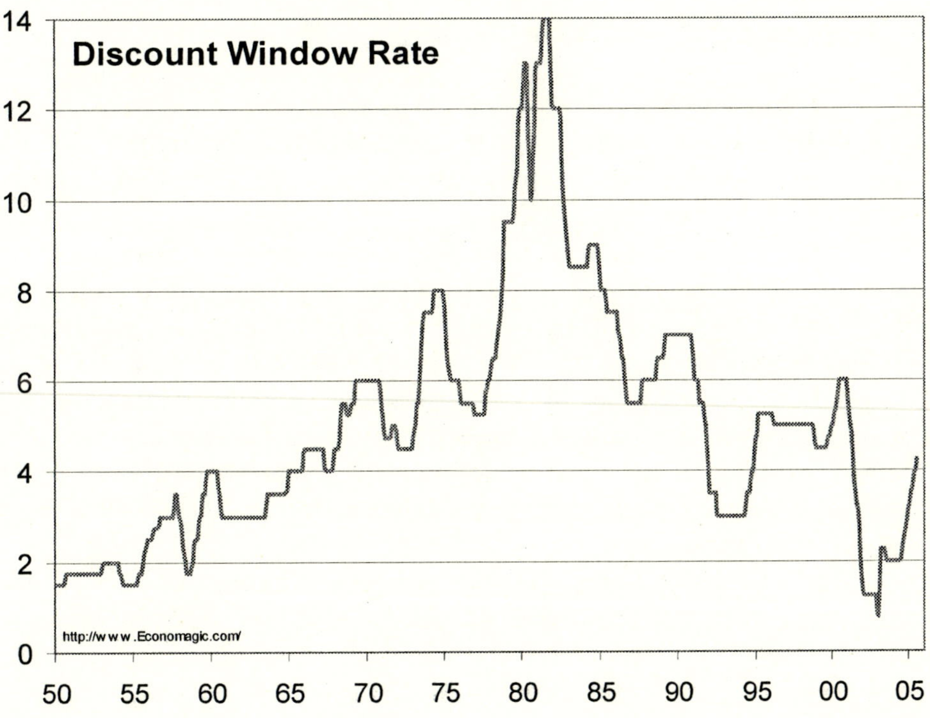

As you can see from these charts, money was cheap and still is. The Federal Reserve gave the economy a real booster shot with these low rates, which kept the overall economy humming along despite the devastating effect of the losses in such a widely-participated-in stock market, which may otherwise have sent the economy into a severe recession, possibly even a depression.

As they say, a recession is when your neighbor is out of work; a depression is when *you* are out of work.

Timing is important; buying deals when they make sense as far as cash flow is important; using leverage wisely helps reduce the risk associated with investment property; having the ability to improve properties and create value is key.

The market for investment property in the New York area was on fire in 2003 and 2004. For the most part, anyplace within an hour or two of the city was not fitting our criteria as far as return on investment. We had to expand our area of focus if we wanted to continue to grow. That is how we ended up in Springfield and Holyoke, Massachusetts. At the time, the deals there were showing a 12 percent cap rate. We figured we had hit the jackpot. Within a few months we were under contract with most of the larger deals that were for sale, or we at least had offers on them.

I was busy lining up the partners, finding the deals and negotiating them, speaking with the Realtors, talking with the banks to line up financing, crunching the numbers, and anything else that popped up to make it all happen. At this stage of the game Den was keeping an eye on our New York properties and doing the various inspections on the deals in Massachusetts. But that all changed mid-sentence. We were in Holyoke doing an inspection on a 48-unit package we had under contract when we found out about a 56-unit package in Springfield that was about to go into foreclosure and we moved on it.

It turns out that the owner had purchased the buildings about three years prior. He was the head maintenance man for a couple of hardworking Russians that had owned the building for several years. He seemed like a hard worker, and I guess the owners felt comfortable with him because he was Russian as well. They did a deal with him for little or no money down for the package. As I am told, once he closed, it was like he hit the lotto. He went out that month and bought a Mercedes, a boat, and went to Florida a few times. He paid the mortgage note, but I think that was about it. Most of the other bills were severely delinquent. He also let the building go as far as maintenance and quality of tenants.

By the time we found out about it, the city of Springfield was ready to start the process of putting the building in receivership. The previous owners had taken the building back by a deed-in-lieu of foreclosure. They did not want to deal with the 450+ violations on the building and the tenants that had basically taken over. They were fed up and trying to sell the building to someone before things got too hairy. We were told there were some deadlines put in place from the city and the clock was ticking. We ended up buying the 64 units for $1,100,000 within less than two weeks of finding out about it. The sellers would hold a small note for 12 months; the rest we needed to come up with in 10 days. This was the roughest two weeks of our lives. It happened so fast that we barely had a chance to think about what was going on. We needed close to $800,000 in a matter of days. Most people we asked thought we were nuts. We were giving good terms:

- a preferential return of profits of 6 to 10 percent;
- a 49 percent split in the potential profits (which was more than usual for us to give the investing partners, for by now we were giving them 24 percent equity).

The main thing was we were buying 64 units for $1,100,000, which came out to only $17,187 a unit. Granted, the buildings needed a lot of work due to three years of neglect. We figured there was $5,000 to $10,000 per unit in upside if we could stabilize the deal. This would turn into a handsome profit to the investing partners, which they would have a split in if the buildings were stabilized and liquidated.

Within that 10 days we had many issues pop up that took hours and hours to deal with. If you think about it, we were cramming into 10 days what normally takes three to six months. The building was heated by gas, but I thought to have the old underground oil tank tested, and sure enough, it had been leaking. This triggered a spill number with the DEC. This set off a whole new round of negotiations, going back and forth with who would pay for the tank removal and who would pay for the cleanup, and up to what amount. There were issues on top of issues. Den and I went to the code-enforcement office and sat down with them for an overview. They were happy to see someone coming in that showed promise, but were skeptical that we could actually pull it off. They showed us a thick file on the property and told us it would not be easy, but they would give us time to get things done. Then there was the matter of insurance; forming the LLC and writing the operating agreements; and surveys and title work to be complete, which everyone had to pull strings in order to get done in time. It was a marathon deal, and I think at one point I had a mild heart attack or something like it. I had to go sit in our conference room for 20 minutes; I was actually seeing stars.

We finally put all the pieces together and closed on the deal. That is when our real work began. Things have never been the same for poor Denny. He talked one of our best workers into moving to Massachusetts to help run the buildings. Carlos had moved from White Plains to Poughkeepsie with his wife and two children and was living in one of our buildings, taking care of it, and working with us on the Poughkeepsie properties. Den has a lot of faith in Carlos. When something needs to be done, all he has to do is tell Carlos and he will work all night if necessary. So they started right in on the violations, having an inspection every few weeks by the code enforcement. It took a few months and a lot of money, but they cleared them all! I remember every few weeks the head of code enforcement would come and Den would have Dunkin Donuts and coffee ready for them. Once the violations were all cleared, we started to focus on the tenants.

Unlike anywhere else that I am aware of, the landlord court system in western Massachusetts heavily favors the tenant. There are crazy statutes in there that aid tenants who are behind in their rent, beat the landlord out of the back rent, and even, by making allegations of neglected repairs (whether true or not), ask the landlord to pay the tenant money for damages. The tenant has no cost or obligation to these attorneys; therefore they have nothing to lose and only time to gain, as opposed to paying their rent by dragging it out in court. The attorneys just hang around the courthouse and ask the tenants who are being evicted if their apartment is in good condition or if there are any problems. We've had tenants sign a statement acknowledging that the apartment is in good condition, and in court, under oath, the tenant denied they ever signed it. Then, when asked again, the tenant admitted that she did indeed sign it but did not read it.

One attorney who works for a firm that specializes in representing tenants even went knocking on doors in one of our buildings looking for clients. The only way this firm stays in business is through representing tenants and, in our cases, making several completely false accusations regarding neglected repairs or anything else they can come up with.

Another insanely written statute claims that if a tenant so chooses, through their own determination, that their apartment is in need of repair, they can stop paying rent. Oddly enough, there is no mention as to actually keeping this withheld rent money in a safe place or even proving it is being set aside, or even proving these damages or items in need of repair are the landlord's fault. In the majority of our cases, the tenant has caused the damage.

I can understand if an apartment is neglected by a landlord, but I can assure you that that's not the case with Delking. We have a 24-hour emergency number with two people on call to handle any problems. These loopholes for tenants encourage bad ethics and a very deceitful way of life, which I cannot wait to get as far away from as possible and never look back.

If the playing field were at all level, we would have continued to invest in the area and continue what we do best: Make buildings look pretty, spend money on repairs, and improve neighborhoods through caring for our property. We purchased six properties in Massachusetts, which consisted of 14 buildings or 132 units, and are selling them all. We have done enough repairs to force a good amount of appreciation as well as improved the tenants and cleared all the violations on the buildings. It's not a total grand slam; for the amount of stress and energy that went into it, our time and energy may have been better directed, but there should be a nice profit for our partners and us.

Florida, on the other hand, was a sweetheart of a deal. We were searching high and low in the Hollywood Beach area for a deal. There were a few to be had in the tail end of 2003, but not many. Things were just about to heat up in the beach and boardwalk area, but not just yet. That whole push away from the major metropolis thing we spoke about earlier was just about to hit Hollywood Beach like a tidal wave.

Our theory is to look as close to a major city as we can get and still find a deal that meets our criteria. This is not easy, but has worked well for us. Springfield is the third-largest city in Massachusetts and about an hour and a half from Boston and 20 to 30 minutes from Hartford, Connecticut. We figure that sooner or later—hopefully sooner—it will spring into a spurt like Poughkeepsie. The same sort of general concept applied to Hollywood Beach. It is 20 to 30 minutes from Miami and 15 minutes from Ft. Lauderdale, and some things were priced like they were in Timbuktu.

We settled in on The St. Maurice Inn, which sits one building in from the boardwalk and beach. It was a 30-unit inn that needed a good deal of work. We really had to stretch ourselves in order to acquire this one. The current owner had a conduit loan that could not be prepaid without a huge penalty, so it had to be assumed. We needed to come up with $800,000 for the rest of the purchase price. The fact that a purchaser needed to come up with more than 50 percent of the purchase price in cash was probably the reason this property was still on the market. These conduit loans do not allow second mortgages. Even so, it was a deal we could not pass up.

Despite the fact that both the exterior and interior of the buildings needed plenty of attention, we had to assume a mortgage with a rate of almost 9 percent or pay a heavy prepayment penalty—almost

$300,000 if we were to pay it off. So we had to come up with a huge down payment. It still had loads of hidden value attached to it. For one thing, we were paying only $50,000 a unit for ocean-side property, while all along the beach units were selling for more than $100,000 a pop. We also realized that by the sign on the front door, which listed the hours of operation as 12 to 2 p.m. and 4 to 6 p.m., the current owner was completely fed up with running the business. This illustrates my earlier point, regarding the difference between owning a business and running a business. The current owner was also running the business, which can be very tiring. With all this in mind, Den and I were still willing to bite. We took a bridge loan for a few hundred thousand and refinanced everything we could.

The deal went through almost immediately, and we improved the property and hired new staff. The managers, Luc and Denise, run the St. Maurice as though it were their own property, always taking care of maintenance issues that pop up and handling the front desk and the particulars with confidence and ease, which has helped to increased business.

Shortly after we purchased the St. Maurice, an all-out land grab began in Hollywood Beach. The red-hot condo fever that was stretching up the coast from Miami and encouraging builders to put up larger and larger condo developments on the beach had just about exhausted all the available oceanfront property. It was as though we were on the cusp of a building frenzy. In talking with neighboring property owners, there was a real excitement in the air.

The Hollywood CRA (Community Redevelopment Agency) is currently moving forward with an all-out improvement in the beach area. They have planned a beatification project for the boardwalk and beach area. By going to http://www.hollywoodbeachcra.org you can see the planned improvements. They even have a slide show of the before-and-after sketches of their proposal, which basically illustrates that over time they will take a 1950s setting and turn it into a posh Palm Beach–type atmosphere, with a cobblestone boardwalk lined with cafés and shops.

Meanwhile, back in Poughkeepsie, the retired lieutenant colonel who had sold us our first two buildings called us because he had decided to sell his last apartment building. They said they did not call anyone else, just us. They wanted $775,000 for the 14-unit building, which was smack in the middle of the city. That came out to $55,357 a unit. The cap rate was just over 10 percent. They must have felt comfortable with us, because they offered to hold a second mortgage for $300,000, which enabled us to get into the deal with just about 10 percent down. The rents in this building were about $200 per unit per month under-market. That would equal an extra $2,800 per month in net income.

This is the deal at purchase:

Purchase price: $775,000
Gross income: $112,000
Net income: $ 75,067
Cap rate: 10%

Down payment: $75,000 + $10,000 (closing cost) = $85,000

Net after mortgage: $11,200
Cash-on-cash return: 13%

We were willing to make an exception to our criteria on this deal because of a few reasons. First of all, we were getting into the deal for about 10 percent, which was a smart use of leverage. Second, we knew the rents were severely under-market; as you will see in the next example, the returns were not going to stay at that level for long. Finally, we knew the owner took good care of his buildings, so the deferred maintenance would not be too overwhelming.

Deal after rent increase:

Purchase price: $775,000
Gross income: $132,700
Net income: $ 95,767
Cap rate: 12.35%

Down payment: $75,000 + $10,000 (closing cost) = $85,000

Net after mortgage: $31,900
Cash-on-cash return: 37.5%

As you can see, the cash-on-cash return, after just a few months of ownership, jumped considerably. We did a few improvements, waited a few months after closing, then raised the rents on the current tenants $100 a month. This is a big jump, but it is still well below the market rent in the area. A few tenants left—one was buying a house, and another was the super, whom we had to evict because he was not keeping his end of the agreement. On these we were able to go up more than just the $100 a month. The best part about the deal was that by improving the net income on the property, we increased the value of the building. A jump in the net income of $20,700 extrapolated into roughly $207,000 to $295,000. The difference depends on the capitalization rate. Valued at a 10 percent cap, the jump in value would be $207,000. At a 7 percent cap, the jump would be $295,000. (If you valued the whole building at a 7 percent cap on the new numbers, it would work out to $1,368,000 or a jump of $593,000 in a matter of months.)

These are powerful, powerful returns. Using the more conservative 10 percent cap rate, which is the capitalization rate we purchased it for, the four-month return on cash invested is 243 percent, not including any of the cash flow and principal paydown.

Let's talk further about the principal paydown on this deal. After all, this does add to the overall return. Our criteria does not work into the enhanced return, because of principal paydown, but it's nice to know it's happening anyway.

Here is what the two mortgages look like:

- 1st mortgage = $400,000 @ 7.05% interest amortized over 20 years.
- Our last payment was for $3,113.21.
- Of that amount, $2,336.47 was interest and $776.74 was principal.

Each month the portion applied to principal goes up and the interest portion goes down with a self-amortizing loan. Let's just take the $776.74 principal paydown and annualize it to $9,320.88. This is now equity in the building, built up through the cash flow from the tenants rent payments. It represents 10.96 percent on our original $85,000 spent on the purchase.

2nd mortgage = \$300,000 @ 7% amortized over 30 years.
Our last payment was for \$1,995.91.

Of that amount, \$1,745.67 was interest and \$250.24 was principal.

If we annualize the principal paydown on the second mortgage, we get \$3,002 or 3.5 percent of our \$85,000 spent on the purchase. (To access amortization charts, go to www.bankrate.com.)

Let's add up the cash flow and the principal paydown:

Cash flow, annual: \$31,900
Cash-on-cash return: 37.5%
1st mortgage annual principal paydown: \$ 9,320 10.96% on cash down
2nd mortgage annual principal paydown: \$ 3,002 3.5% on cash down

One way to look at the returns of this purchase would be to take all these into account, bringing the total annual return to 51.96 percent. Or you could take the point of view that since the improved net income created an additional \$207,000 (in appreciation) or 243 percent of the \$85,000 used to purchase the property, that that is the return. However you slice it, leverage played a large part in amplifying the return. It must also be noted that there is no assurance that all the rents will be collected or that we won't be hit with a large repair bill, thus reducing the cash flow. Worst of all, valuations or capitalization rates may come down, causing the building to depreciate. But if depreciation were to come into play, we would have some protection or a buffer in that we have that extra net income to cushion the fall.

Let's say cap rates dropped. Below is the value of the building at a 12 percent cap rate on the new numbers:

Net income: $ 95,767
Cap rate: 12%
Price would be: $798,000

As Scott Jerutis likes to say, by finding deals that we can add value to, we are "Buffettizing" the real estate market. That is, taking the principals that Warren Buffet uses in the stock market and applying it to the real estate market. We are looking for inefficiencies that can be found if investigated thoroughly. I do believe that over time, these inefficiencies will become less easy to find, because of, you guessed it, the Internet. Websites like www.Loopnet.com, which enables users to search through thousands of available deals all over the country in seconds, will help to level the playing field for the small investor. That does not mean it will be impossible to find deals, but it may make it a bit harder.

Ownership in the apartment industry remains, for the most part, in the hands of the individual investor. The industry is not institutionalized. The top 50 companies own only 18 percent of the country's 16.4 million apartment units. The average capitalization rates of apartments throughout the country are under 7 percent. This simply means that the net income or NOI (which is the income after expenses and before debt service) would have a return of less than 7 percent if the full purchase price was paid for the property. The key is to look hard for deals with inefficiencies: rents below market, underutilized space, buildings in need of repair, and in the case of a business or a motel or hotel, bad management.

Some stats on LoopNet:

LoopNet.com, Inc., is the number one online commercial real estate service, with more commercial property listings, more site traffic and members, and more geographic market coverage than any other company.

Summary

Registered Members	700,000
Properties for Sale	$175 billion
Space for Lease	2.5 billion sq. ft.
Geographic Market Coverage	All U.S. and Canadian markets
User Sessions	2.3 million per month
Average Time Spent on LoopNet	27 minutes
Property Listings Returned in Search Results	60 million per month
Property Listings Viewed	4.5 million per month

Chapter Eighteen
Summing It All Up

"Twenty years from now, you will be more disappointed by things you didn't try than ones you did. So throw off the bowlines. Sail away from the safe harbor. Catch the trade winds in your sale. Explore. Dream. Discover."

– *Mark Twain*

As the co-owner, along with Denio DeLaurentis, of the Delking Group of Companies, which consists of 19 separate LLC's, about 30 buildings, and more than 350 rental units stretching from south Florida up to western Massachusetts, with a total value someplace over $20,000,000, I can honestly say with much conviction that investing in real estate, particularly cash-flow properties, especially with the use of leverage, offers very favorable odds of huge returns, blowing the doors off of other investment asset classes.

A major ingredient to the increased odds is the ability to leverage. As is often the case with commercial deals, you have the ability to purchase a property worth more than two, four, and even ten times your initial capital, or down-payment money. And if the deal is attractive, it's easy enough to take on a partner to help fund larger purchases. Then, with the rents collected, you pay down a mortgage, which in turn creates equity, and a portion of the cash flow can be sheltered from taxes because of depreciation. As I pointed out earlier, even a small amount of appreciation gets amplified in relation to the amount of the down payment.

The best part is, you don't have to be a rocket scientist; you just need to pay attention to simple details, like working through the numbers and making basic assumptions about the property, the location, asking yourself if the rents are below market, and trying to find ways to improve the property.

I felt compelled to tell my story because, first off, I think it can be helpful to someone who is just starting out. I know when I was starting out on Wall Street and in real estate, I would have loved this story or one like it. And second, when I think back and relive the events of the last fifteen years—the ups, the downs, the cycles, the euphoria followed by despair, and then putting it all on the line and venturing into real estate with great success—it really makes me just smile, shake my head, and say, "This should be in a book."

Only in America can someone build up a business, watch it crumble, struggle through some tough times, and manage to build it back up again to the point of doing a million dollars in commission, only to watch it completely fall apart all over again, then with absolutely no cash—I mean, not a dime—pull equity out of a house, and build up another company and then write a (hope-to-be) best-selling book about the whole ordeal. As things stand today, the average national capitalization rate on apartment buildings is under 6.7 percent, so being conservative, if we value all the buildings at a 9 percent cap, Denio's and my portion of the equity is just over $3,000,000 each. If we value them at a 7 percent cap (still less aggressive than the national average), our equity is $4,600,000 each. This would bring the return on the only money I put into the purchase of real estate (the $15,000 in my first home purchase) to between 20,000 percent and 30,000 percent. Through the use of careful leverage, refinancing, utilizing carefully selected investing partners, and catching the real estate market at the right time, we were able to grow our real estate holdings at a phenomenal rate.

Understand, this equity is not like money in the bank, as anyone who saw their brokerage account swell to eye-popping levels and then implode during the good old Internet bubble can attest to. Things can change on a dime. The good thing about having gone through that time is that we know sooner or later trends change. We can only hope that by following our motto of sticking with cash-flow deals and making sure that the properties we purchase have the ability to be improved somehow, we will stay out of harm's way.

Below is a chart from economagic.com of single-family home prices sold, going back to 1963. There are thousands of charts and statistics available at www.Economagic.com that you can create and browse through.

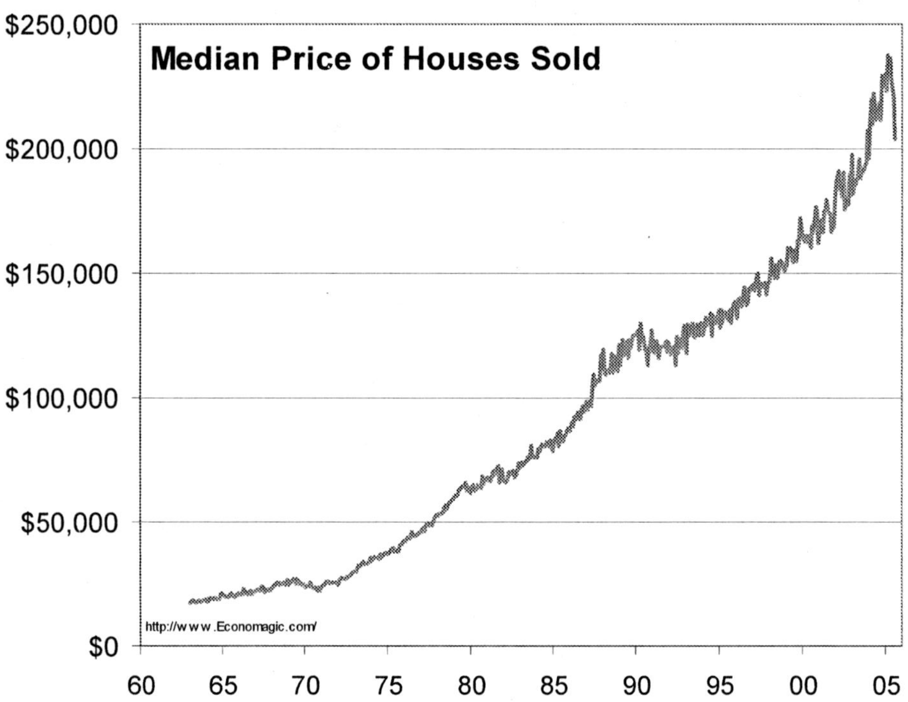

Ted at www.economagic.com was extremely helpful in preparing the chart below (used in the cover) and in allowing me to use his charts in this book.

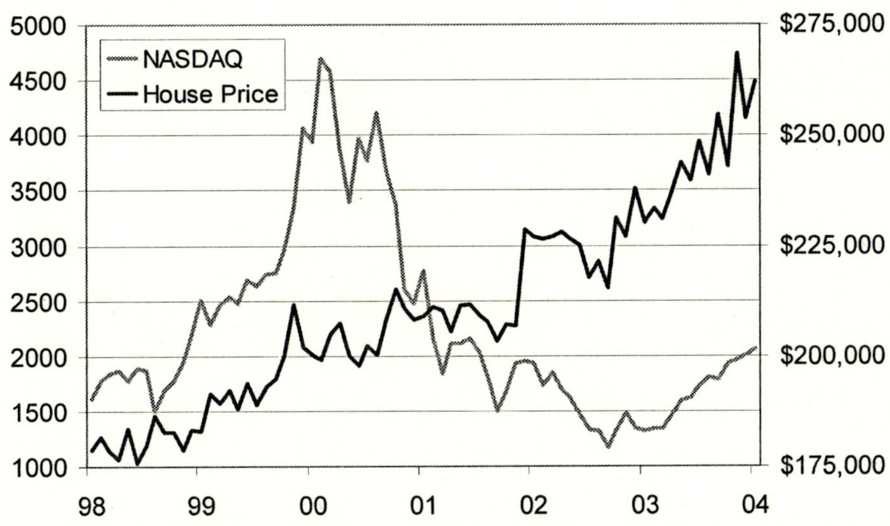

Where the two charts intersect is where I moved from Wall St. into real estate. I hope the information in this book is useful and please remember this is not financial, tax or professional advice. Feel free to contact me with questions at kkingston@delkingmgt.com an keep an eye on my Blog "The Real Estate Investors Blog at: http://www.bloglines.com/blog/KevinKingston

Printed in the United States
45103LVS00007B/5